THE GOSPEL ACCORDING TO THOMAS

EVENT HORIZON
PUBLISHING, LLC

The Gospel According to
THOMAS

The Gospel According To **THOMAS**

To the Soul of William Samuel :

*T*HANK YOU FOR BEING AHEAD OF YOUR TIME -
BY BRINGING BACK THE 'ANCIENT OF DAYS' TRUTH-TEACHINGS,
AND WISDOM.

REVIEWS

This book brought me up-to-date on spiritual developments since 1945, when a document find (called the 'Nag Hammadi Library') was discovered. Until now the importance of it was greatly underplayed. Laying dormant, preserved in unadulterated purity for centuries, this treasure's true value lies deep within its unexplored meaning. I was amazed and elevated in reading the hidden meanings contained in Christ's words and teachings interpreted here by Lachlen French. His interpretation is bliss! No wonder it's been #1 on Amazon!

~ G.R. Rankin, Illustrator / Book Designer

I really love this book, *The Gospel According to Thomas*. I have read other author's on this same subject, but this one is very special, as Lachlen French has taken the words and history to a truly transcendent level of understanding. Mr. French has a gift for seeing the Light of Truth behind the words, for seeing the metaphysical and subjective meanings of the words that Yeshua spoke. This is brilliant. Here we find a way to really understand the subjective, non-dual vision that was taught by Yeshua; the secret teachings that were 'left out' of the Bible. You will come away from this book truly enlightened at a very deep level. This is an important book. It's more than history; this is a guide back to Understanding, Self-discovery and Peace.

~ Sandy Jones, Author – Barefoot at Heart, CA Bookseller

Mr. French is a superlative researcher and writer. Beyond earlier attempts by others to present the writings of Thomas, this author has not only presented the pieces and fragments in correct orderly fashion, but manages to bring to the teachings both a spiritual and emotional dimension. Not only is it a superb piece of scholarly work but a truly inspirational rendering that far exceeds the dry but scholarly works that preceded it.

~ Michael Lanier, Former Chief Executive

DEDICATIONS

*"Every man takes the limits of his own field of vision
  for the limits of the world."*

Arthur Schopenhauer

"The mind's direction is more important than its progress."

Joseph Joubeart

*"Dogma does not mean the absence of thought, but the
end of thought.*

Gilbert Keith Chesterton

*"It were not best that we should all think alike;
  it is a difference of opinion that makes horse races."*

Mark Twain

*"Most of one's life is one's prolonged effort to prevent
  oneself thinking."*

Aldous Leonard Huxley

"Colleges hate geniuses just as convents hate saints."

Ralph Waldo Emerson

"Be careful how you interpret the world: It is like that."

Erich Heller

BY LACHLEN PAUL FRENCH:

God, Einstein, Existence, Cosmos, Life, Love, You

Christ's Mystic Secret Returns

Darwin's Fatal Admission

Breath of Light

Splendorous Light Within

Gospel According to Thomas
A MODERN VERSION AMPLIFIED AND INTERPRETED FOR TODAY

Mystic Traveler I, II, III

Aquarian Effect

TABLE OF CONTENTS

~ *The Ancient* "Emerald Tablet" ~
(In the Beginning...and even Now)

What is Below (in the physical, and earthly expression)
is like that Above (the Divine Source).
What is Above (the Heavenly Creative Consciousness),
is Similar, to That below (the subservient Earthly Manifestation)
...to accomplish the wonders of The One.
As all things were produced by
the mediation of The One Being,
So all things were produced from The One...
in continuing adaptation.
It is the cause of all Perfection throughout...
Separate the Earth (the bodily identification)
from the Fire (the elevating Breath)
And segregate the Subtle (the Soul's Vision)
from the Gross, (from the ego-persona)
and act Prudently (holding serenely In Consciousness, Your Truth).
Then, with Discernment, Ascend with the greatest Sagacity,
From the Earth (from your lower earthly perspective)
Up to Heaven (up to your Creative, Heavenly Consciousness)
And then... with Resolution... descend again to Earth.

UNITE together the power of things inferior, with SUPERIOR
Thus... you will possess the Light of the whole world...
And all Obscurity will fly away from you.
All Untoward Conditions and Confusion will Melt Away from your life.
This Knowledge has more Fortitude than fortitude itself,
because it will overcome every subtle thing (every causal force)...
and it will Penetrate... every solid thing
(all material manifestations).
By This path, the world was formed."

Adapted from — The Emerald Tablet of '*Hermes Trismagistus*' – aka: <u>Enoch</u>
(parentheses are mine, bold is the original)

SUBLIME ONENESS

There is a vast, unplumbed inner world .. that we may find,
that we may reach .. haply, haltingly, yet gracefully ..
that when visited .. exults our being, in shared Auras;
Yet our sensibilities are Dismayed as well.

In this "elevated depth within" a Vibrational Permeation
deeply penetrates us .. and purifies our old self images
of their coherence .. their cohesion. And our Identity herein,
becomes Pure Unfettered Simplicity – of being.

This vast Inner experience restores to us 'Knowing our Heritage'
(as in a dream .. faintly remembered).
It energizes a Deep Awareness in us .. of our Eternity,
and grants us Feelings .. that ne'er were touched.
The amplification In and Of our Being .. in this rarified Knowing,
lights ancient memories of our Original SELF
(as an identity from above) .. somewhere .. somehow.
Yet .. finally, we are Hollowed out .. we are Emptied;
but we are filled with a glory of some Heavenly Sun,
.. barely seen later, in the 'afterglows remembered'.

But we DO remember feeling absolute Surrender in the face
of an All Consuming Love; and we feel an unyielding deferential Awe
in wordless jubilation .. that we've even FELT such Tenderness.
Forever after we are changed.

We are always looking for its surprises around endless corners,
over hills .. in other fields and byways.
We Often feel its marbled essence and apparitions,
maybe Here, maybe There, and Yonder .. and often at night.

YES feeling it, sensing it, it is like a fond invisible touch on our skin
or a lovely Aromatic Essence – a sort of ever-present FRAGRANCE
Of Grace .. blessing our Awareness .. Promising its next visitation.

It's felt especially in our deeply conscious breath and breathing,
for OUR breath, is ITS etheric Essence -- Invisible, Powerful.
Yes, it actually Permeates our being .. AS Our Being;
(being only .. a Consciousness of Loving Life).

So finally .. never releasing its Love .. we also become,
its Compassioned and Passionate Ambassador.

-- *Lachlen French* --

~ PREFACE ~

THE MYSTERY OF THE AGES
"COMES TO TOWN"

Human history contains a spiritual secret. It was known by the ancient ruling elite, but the masses of humanity never received it. Now, it's been buried for so long almost no one has it, but ardent seekers and the truly sincere – who realize its power. Yet deep within each of us we know it in a subliminal way. It's felt in our dreams. Our hearts know it and long for it, because of fond silent memories, somewhere inside. Quietly yearning for a tender lifting-love we have mysterious remembrances in our twilight consciousness - in going to sleep, in rising or in meditation. We unknowingly look for its serenity in cascading messages of *Belonging,* that we somehow feel. Our heart knows its truth – that there is something infinitely higher – behind, and one-with our essential Livingness.

This exquisite reality within, is the birthplace of our private states of inexplicable elevated euphoria. And when humanity seeks pleasure in altered states with unhealthy substances or food stuffing, we're engaging an Ersatz chemical euphoria, with lazy or poor choices. It's why people enjoy the substance-methods as a shortcut, because they allow respite from ego's pain (as an *inner bliss of Connection* is felt from *something* divine). Artificial methods for touching this inner reverie actually *bypass* our true heavenly pathway to it, within. Yet there's a True experience and wondrous reality that is so far above this ego-life (especially the euphoria from substance abuse) that nothing of this life can even approach it. It is like comparing a candle to The Sun.

We provide a name for this inner reality inside us; that in fact transforms our comprehension of personal identity – we have termed it: the **God Experience.**

Whether we know it or not *Yeshua* (his name in *Hebrew* which we will be using herein), known as *Iesous* (in *Greek*), *Isa* (in Aramaic) and *Jesus* (in *Latin*), came offering us this legendary God Experience, which yields the pure and natural aspects of inner bliss and personal power. His promise of power is all but forgotten. *Yeshua – Iesous – Isa – Jesus* said we would do greater works than he, applying his Holy Breath (Spirit) discipline that he offered privately to his disciples outside organized religiosity.

Religion keeps The God Experience hidden. Yeshua's secret truth was covered up so fully by church ritual that its blessed intent was lost for millennia. Religion ceremonialized Yeshua's spiritual discipline, so its power's been unknown (essentially making it *a non-event*). His mission however was to share the Blissful Power through The God Experience which he intended to benefit all (*for anyone who's willing to become it*). The book in your hand gives the elevated words, principles and teachings so we may come to know and feel this inner power and truth, daily.

THE GOSPEL ACCORDING TO THOMAS

In this regard many have not heard that another gospel of Christ was newly discovered in the 20th century - words spoken to his closest disciples in private. It is said that more than 95+ percent of the world's population did not hear we found this new gospel, among 45 other Christian documents in a earthen jar in 1945, where it had lain buried, hidden for nearly 2,000 years in sand, close to Yeshua's country. This indicates *other* gospels existed alongside those four gospels that were placed in Emperor Constantine's Roman Bible 400 years later, in 381 CE (Common Era). We now know there were scroll-cache's called the *'Essene' and 'Nag-Hammadi' Libraries* that the Roman army thankfully never found or got to assimilate when destroying the nation of Israel (*taking literally everything for processing-control* of all Israelite artifacts) back to Rome's treasuries.

This newly discovered gospel is reportedly written by Yeshua' brother no less, Didymus Judas Thomas, one of the sons of Joseph and Mary and one of Yeshua' 12 apostles. This document *The Gospel According to Thomas*, is being honored and studied worldwide and has been for decades. It's been analyzed by scholars in books, on radio, even TV talk shows, also at seminaries, universities and international spiritual retreats.

THE 1940'S DISCOVERIES

In 1945 to 1947 two awe-inspiring ancient archeological discoveries *changed* the face of what we know of spiritual history. Many are simply not aware of it. A remarkable aspect regarding both of these discoveries is that each is a Find hidden in sand for almost 2,000 years. They are such ancient documents that no one touched them for millennia. Are they *interesting?* Yes! We now find that we've been taught a religious bedtime story for thousands of years, and this knowledge has *changed* everything.

The Gospel According To Thomas is like listening to Yeshua talk to *US* around a campfire - like he's speaking directly to us in a first-person communication style. The *Nag-Hammadi Library* and *The Essene Library* at Qumran, Israel near the Dead Sea (*essentially Unknown by most people for half a century*) now reveal the true facts and the real story.

Did you know that the four gospels in the Bible were written by various folks writing many decades later, *after Yeshua?* Thomas was probably composed while Yeshua was there - according to some experts. Then was "lost" for a few millennia, yet was re-discovered in 1945. This uncovering was "earth-shaking" and shocking - (*perhaps intended)?*

It made religious figures uncomfortable - at least terribly curious. What did we find? The quotations of Christ in Thomas are so similar to the four gospels that some experts claim that Thomas may be the long lost "Q"- "source scroll" from which the quotations of Christ in Matthew, Mark and Luke came.

This other ancient discovery that almost everyone has heard of is the Essene Library (*the Dead Sea Scrolls*). These documents included the whole Old Testament except for Esther. Also present, were other spiritual scrolls and treatises from a truly wise spiritual people.

The other documents in that cache' **strangely and inexplicably resemble quotations from Yeshua in the Bible's four gospels**. The strange thing? They were written hundreds of years before Christ was born. *How could that be?* Well, Yeshua was quoting them, as he obviously studied them.

What if the story told us for 2000 years was not supported by the most ancient millennia-old newly discovered documents - documents whose veracity in their carbon dated origins, *change what we've been told* for millennia? It's like finding "*newspapers* from 2000 years ago".

Now, awhile after the Essene's Dead Sea Scrolls were announced as *'just discovered'* Catholic authorities immediately sent seven scholars to evaluate these finds. Why would they not do so? Of course they would. Despite powerful similarities to the Bible's gospels and the Old Testament biblical books, aspersions were cast on all these incredible discoveries in the 1940's. *Why?* Why not do so? To esteem them, well.. it throws a *wrench* in the works. *"Better to keep the status quo".* These scholars secreted away several of these Essene Dead Sea Scrolls though, and have kept them from the rest of our eyes all this time. Why, I wonder?

You'll be interested to know that the Essenes were the third primary Jewish sect of Yeshua's day. The Pharisees and Sadducees were the other two. Those two others are both seen in the New Testament story. Yeshua was raised Essene. They were the spiritual transcribers of the day. They transcribed endless copies of the Old Testament and their own remarkable spiritual documents too, and sent them far and wide across the land.

THE OTHER GUYS

When *Yeshua* came out to teach his fellow Israelites he was delivering an Ancient of days truth-teaching on the present, imminent and eminent nature of God, and of the ecstatic interior pathway for a divine relationship. This was the ancient truth teaching of *Abraham, Isaac, Jacob, and the High Priest Zadok,* and the teachings that King David was privy to.

See, the Essenes were very private. They had communities and villages apart from the rest of the world. They lived their spirituality in real privacy, and did not give themselves challenges to deal with in 'outer' worldly issues and matters, in societal interaction. So the Essenes were basically unfamiliar to everyone - who was not an Essene. No one really knew their teachings, or values – except that they loved privacy.

Of course *all the citizenry* of Israel were basically Jewish in their spiritual beliefs, and were *all* children of Abraham, and also followed *Mosaic* Law in the Torah (the first 5 books of the Bible) so everyone assumedly believed that the Essenes were believers and adherents to Judaism of course.

But every sect had its own uniqueness; for example, the Sadducees did not believe in an afterlife; the Pharisees were strict *Do's & Don'ts doers,* even incorporated silly requirements and foolish strictures in adherence, producing self-righteousness, as they were trying to outdo others in their strict forms of righteousness; but all it did was make them value-judgmental against everyone else, and condescending in general. They were imperiously self-righteous and hard to live with. Yeshua found dealing with them a real entertainment, yet a challenge to his patience as well.

ESSENE SPIRITUALITY AND TEACHING

The remarkable fact about ancient Essene documents in the Essene Library, in Israel, *discovered 1947* is they reveal a true and deeply felt Experience of God for their disciple-adherents. We can now see why the message of Christ was so popular - so *moving*. We may now understand how the birth of a World Religion occurred with such authority! The message and its promises of real power in the Individual were so extraordinary it would be impossible to ignore.

As said, there were 2 sides to Israel's spirituality. One side was represented by many groups and Jewish sects, who had a *letter of the law, holier than thou approach,* which engendered self righteousness. The other side of spirituality was represented essentially by the Essenes practicing holiness - reverence in moment to moment living, by partnering with God in their individual daily life-consciousness. This was making the Divine ONE a partner in every second of the day. Yes, it's challenging to remember it in every moment, but we have our entire life to practice, they would say.

Known as a Race of Priests in a *New Covenant* with God the Essenes did not call themselves the foreign word 'Essene'. They called themselves the *Sons of Zadok,* after King David's high priest. Everyone of the Essenes was to become so enlightened - dedicating their life to living in God's interior essence, that they could be teacher, healer, priest if ever called upon. This whole spiritual philosophy was dedicated to consciously living.. for.. with.. and *In* God's inner personal Presence. This was Christ's message .. and activity; bringing God closer - not more distant - but more present.

The Essene *Teacher of Righteousness,* whoever he was, started this group-teaching circa 200 BCE. His anonymity is one of the great historical mysteries of all worldwide spiritual movements. In fact, he was teaching Abraham's righteousness, which is *listening for the guidance of God in consciousness to obey it.* This Teacher showed a way to practice hearing God's voice in a spiritual manner - to follow the wisdom. This allows a divine destiny for each life. By hearing God's leading, we see its natural grace. To find this partnership, we go deeply within, and then our heart magically knows its truth. Our life may then personify a divine human life. This was Yeshua' path.

Yeshua (Yeshua) was born in the first century BCE. Yeshua' birth is thought to be near 7 to 6 BCE. His crucifixion is thought to have occurred about 38 years later. Yeshua was raised as an *Essene,* although biblical gospels do not reveal it. We know all this because Yeshua was quoting essene spiritual scrolls that were written by them, but never put in the Bible by the Roman Emperor Constantine, a Mithraite pagan, a Syrian offshoot of Zoroastrianism. He did not "convert" till his last breath of life.

When Yeshua spoke beautiful truth-principles like *"Let not the sun go down on your wrath"; or The Meek shall inherit the Earth." or "Turn the other cheek";* he was quoting Essene writings that Emperor Constantine either chose to leave out (*because it revealed Yeshua was quoting some other material)* or because he never acquired the documents, as they'd been hidden. **Baptism** as a celebratory and yet quite serious ritual of "dying to one's Old Life" and being "resurrected" to a spiritual life again (*from the watery grave of immersion in deep water)* WAS an Essene ritual and practice. The other sects did not practice baptism. John the Baptist and Yeshua were baptizing people into a deep Essene teaching and lifestyle of inner oneness with God - in their consciousness and momentary life. The Pharisees and Sadducees of Yeshua' time were set at odds with him, continually arguing with him and John the Baptist - who was Yeshua's cousin, and Essene too. Their antagonistic plans for *Yeshua-Yeshua* became a feverish endeavor. They had both Yeshua and John killed, in fact.

Because the Essenes were unknown as a group *(in beliefs or differences)* not many could explain anything about them. Yet the wonderful thing was their fame spread near and far – not their beliefs, but their lifestyle. Living AWAY from the world, trading *among themselves,* helping each member of the community in regular, and even unfortunate times or circumstances, their '*love of their fellowman as a way of life*' became well-known to famous historians of the time.

Philo the Greek historian commentator, said "*beg them to come out to us and teach us their gospel of peace and freedom."* The famous Josephus even lived with Essenes for 3 years and wrote on their deep spiritual dedication, their daily practices and wrote on their ancientness. Pliny also wrote saying how "*they're a race by themselves and remarkably different from all others in the whole wide world. They live without money, and for companionship they have palm trees; they have existed for thousands of generations."*

Well, they had each other as well, and they really had God too, *in heart and mind,* whom they loved ardently in all their daily conscious pursuits and practices. And this was the path Yeshua was raised within and taught.

INTRODUCTION

IS THERE A MEANING TO ALL OF THIS WORLD EXPERIENCE?

Yeshua's *teaching* of his Essene principles made him popular. He taught the wondrous and deeply satisfying partnership-experience with God, and his influence expanded. Being perhaps the most powerful, loving and charismatic Essene Rabbi in their whole group made him perfect for '*coming out to the outside world'* and sharing, and teaching everyone this truly spiritual interior path of making the Divine ONE a partner in momentary living. People felt and could see the beauty of genuine inner spirituality.

By contrast, the old religious forms and rituals were lifeless - unsatisfying. The Pharisees *do's and don'ts* were boring. Whenever people get to experience the ecstatic experience of God within themselves, the're convinced of Christ's truth-teaching. Their ego melts away for a tangible time of transformational deep awareness and they realize that they are one-with lighted, lifting, fiery, beloved, healing, infinite Divine Being.

That there is pure inexhaustible bliss as part of its natural experiential state, makes it irresistible to us. Competing with Yeshua' and John's view of spirituality the other religious sects began to see Yeshua as subversive of their public influence. Yeshua and John The Baptist's new Essene movement, was growing. Whenever anyone gets to realize '*I can have boring ineffective religiosity, or I can experience the highest sublime ego-melting light, love and awe-filled God Experience - I know which one to pick from now on'*. They'll pick the divine path inside. One never forgets its grace. The poem on page 13 describes this.

Shortly after Yeshua's departure, the Apostle Paul came on the scene preaching much of this beautiful message. An interesting fact is that Paul being a learn'ed man and able communicator began writing his Epistles before everyone had else started writing, almost. *Thomas* probably had him beat for the 'first writing'.

Many people think that because the Gospels come first in New Testament order, they were written before Paul's epistles (as if he had them to peruse). Not true. They were written 20-70 years later. Paul did not have a New Testament to study nor even a consolidated Old Testament. The canon of Old Testament books were agreed to by Hebrew scholars of that day, yes, but they were not published like they are now.

Paul may have had the scrolls that were known as '*Thomases*' and many other Essene scrolls too, written over hundreds of years, but we really don't know what he read (except we can say that he *Quoted the Essene scrolls)* the ones that are not even part of the Old Testament (*and put the quotes in his OWN epistles like Galatians, Philippians, Ephesians, Corinthians, etc.*). He quoted and utilized their original thinking quite often.

Paul did not have The four Gospels as an inspiration when he wrote his epistle/letters. The Bible was collated mid-fourth century when Rome decided that spirituality was something to be controlled. Paul's creativity came from elsewhere, and from his own heart. This is why many gospel Topics are not mentioned in Paul's writings - (him writing from a earlier time and purpose) and to different people.

So what did Paul have to study anyway, if anything, other than the Old Testament? With the Essene scrolls at the Dead Sea, at Qumran (koom-rahn) 13 miles from Jerusalem, Paul could travel there in several hours and study their many scrolls at great length, or acquire some for his continuing benefit. He probably carried *The Book of Enoch* around, as it inspired his writing, and was THE most famous spiritual document of the era, everyone studied, quoted and referenced. *It's even quoted in Jude,* yes. These were the documents that Yeshua and John the Baptist studied. The Essenes had perhaps the greatest spiritual library in the ancient world.

The thousands of scrolls and scroll fragments we now possess from the Essenes reveal where Paul picked up phrases like the **new covenant, new testament, sons of light, children of darkness; and the analogies of Sarah and Hagar and the "Heavenly Jerusalem" of the New Covenant.** These word images are prevalent in the *New Testament* (a phrase that *also* came from the Essenes) and they are used in Revelation and Paul's Epistles but they existed 250 years before "Christianity's" rise.

Essene copies of Isaiah, for example, are nearly a thousand years older than the Roman version of Isaiah, and they have 20% more of Isaiah's text in them as originally written; (as it was edited by the Mithraites overseeing its compilation). The Essene biblical scrolls are fresher and unedited – and different from those documents from which we translate Bibles today. *Hmmm.*

Yet only about one third of the spiritual documents were the Old Testament books. The other two thirds were their wisdom scrolls, life-discipline documents, and prophetic treatises—created by their incredibly insightful Masters. It was these Essene Master's writings which the Apostle Paul was utilizing in his 'similar' phrasing. They were bringing new life to spirituality.

After comparing Yeshua's teaching-instruction in spirituality, (*which almost no one knows about today because of the obfuscation of the linguistics by Bible translators)* with the **Essene scrolls found in the Essene Library** at Qumran, Israel, we can now see that, that which survived the first century was the very private spiritual path of the Essene Brotherhood, who called themselves a Race of Priests. Yet, they came to be known as *Christian.* Always remember *Christ and Christianity* are Greek words. Those words "as descriptions" of Yeshua's teaching were connected to the movement very much later - *decades and centuries* later - yet they mean the same as the Hebrew words *Messianists or Messiah.* What does all this mean?

Just know, the Jewish nation and people had been captured, enslaved or conquered for many centuries. All their hopes were based in *a new arising of their nation and its profile in the Mediterranean region*, rising up again like unto the wealthy powerful esteemed days of King David, or King Solomon. The word *Messiah* means Anointed One (meaning a KING) who was anointed like all the kings of Israel were anointed at their coronation. They were anointed with olive oil, perhaps drenched in it, being poured over their head. The prophesies of a new King in a new Time in the future made the people of the nation look forward. They hoped for this new better time and new King. So what did they get?

They got absolutely destroyed as a nation by Rome. Rome slew man, woman and child in 70CE and again with that little remnant in 130CE. Rome swept over the whole land and essentially took everything that had even a *little* value, back to Rome to their treasuries - books, scrolls, money, dining ware, and historical material - to the hall of records for all documents. Many Jews of course fled on wagons, carts, donkeys, and animals before the Roman armies arrived to kill them. So what happened to their prophesies of a Messiah (new king)?

Well, they're now interpreted by people of an *Essene or Christian inclination* AS *YESHUA--Yeshua--Iesous.* He was a new "king in spirituality" and in righteousness, reigning in consciousness for how to live in this dualistic world of good and evil. Of course the Jewish people of today do not see Yeshua (*one of their own--but merely from the Essene faith-sect*) as the promised King at all. Even though the New Testament takes an exceptional amount of time to prove Yeshua's *blood line relation to King David,* Jews did not see a king there in *Iesous* (as Greeks called him). They know he lived and preached there but they know he was crucified too. (Not very Kingly).

But when Yeshua was so powerful, loving, wise and was so transformative of human history, and because he became the most famous individual in world history - known everywhere - and when the Essene movement about oneness with God, *known later as Christianity in the Greek language,* grew like wildfire, becoming powerful in the hearts and minds of many, the Roman empire said, *Uh oh, if we can't beat 'em, we better join them.* And by doing so took over the spiritual movement with buildings, daily services, rituals, ceremonies, costumes, smoke, wafers, wine and liturgies. By organizing it and "taxing" it with offerings and tithes from the folks, the Roman government grew even more wealthy and powerful.

THE TREASURE TROVE FOUND IN ISRAEL REVEALS FACTS

Many people think there was a hollow empty period in Israelite history from 250 BCE onward till Yeshua came on the scene in the New Testament. Not so. It was the Essenes who gave birth to practicing true spirituality studying day and night and meditating for oneness with God-Mind's within. They created inspired documents too, and created spiritual centers and communities in Israel.

Their documents preceded all the Roman scrolls, hundreds of years later. What we can see, is that Rome simply borrowed Israelite scripture and called it, *its own,* controlled it, assimilated it, edited it, and compiled it. But actually, we need to say thank you .. to the Essenes and Yeshua.

This can all be verified by simply studying the Essene scrolls discovered in Israel in the in 1947, which predate Paul the Apostle's writings and the Roman church by many, many hundreds of years. The age, purity and original status of those writings exceed all New Testament codices and scrolls. It was the Essenes who preserved all the older biblical scrolls for posterity creating a library second to none in that era, which included an awareness of all the world's past and current religious thought.

Yeshua was quite cosmopolitan in his spiritual awareness and education – Egyptian, Sumerian, Zoroastrian paths were known by him. The Essene Masters wrote voluminously for two centuries on the Law, the Prophets, and the Writings and other's material too. They conveyed historical and spiritual insights not seen before or after. We can thank them for preserving and sharing the Old Testament all over their land.

Now let's inform our awareness further looking at the geography there. *Sumeria*, 4000 BCE (Iraq-Iran today) preceded *Egypt* as a world power. Egypt's Old Kingdom began 3100 BCE and was considered North Africa and the River Nile. Proto-Indo-European migrations started into Egypt about 5500 BCE. These kingdoms were east and south of Israel.

Their spiritual culture is seen in Moses' knowledge, as he was instructed in Egypt's Royal Mystery Schools which shared foundational roots with Sumeria and other nations. Moses was a prince in Egypt though he was Hebrew, and he thereby absorbed the spiritual education that royalty received. He gave birth to Judaism by coming from Abraham's ancient teachings of the One God everywhere (even in our heart) and the esoteric education he got in Egypt.

Greece ruled and influenced the ancient world for centuries. *Alexander the Great* died in 323-BCE yet conquered-Hellenized *(made like Greece)* the known world - ruling philosophy, language, science, architecture, money in half the world. We can see Greece's influence in our modern cultures in science, philosophy, language, even our Olympics.

When Yeshua was born, most everyone in the Mediterranean world used Greek in speaking, mathematics and writing. The New Testament was created in the Greek language (actually *Koine* [koy-nay) the *common man's Greek-*(because the Greek civilization ran the world in commerce, trading centers and practices). Yet the kingdom split up at Alexander's death and their culture-sharing philosophy faded away. Aramaic was the other language of Yeshua and his people too.

Next, Rome rose up co-opting Greco influence. They copied Greek architecture, military thought, religious and cultural ideology. They added brutal conquest, slavery, monetary and political domination, everywhere they went. At its zenith, Rome exemplified the ugliest most imperialistic, violent taxing-force in history. Their international policy-strategies were universally loathed.

Their daily entertainment delivered slaves from foreign lands to the Coliseum where they were disemboweled with swords by Roman gladiators or ripped apart or eaten by wild animals. After a time, the city of Rome was populated almost entirely by slaves from foreign countries, with no hope at all in their life or their heart; amidst a tiny rich class, that was protected by endless armies-soldiers. For a modern-day analogy of Rome's propensities it would be like having Joseph Stalin, of early Soviet Russia, ruling the world.

After so much of this, Romans became psychologically and spiritually hardened, going deeper into spiritual darkness. In religious public-relations efforts, after crucifying thousands of Christians over hundreds of years, in a worldwide attempt at social acceptance, Rome adopted Christianity because of its growth rate. People became faithful and fearless, by it.

Empires see religion as mass populace control. Co-opting a spiritual movement (*everyone was falling in love-with and was growing noticably*) was a brilliant strategy. The only problem? Rome changed the Message.

They put God over there, and us over here. Divine Infinite Omnipresence was deleted. They gave God toenails, teeth, white hair, knuckles and elbows. They seated him on a marble chair. They made God like a man with an ego-nature. Read here what came from the Nag-Hammadi Library, discovered in 1945 - *John's Secret Gospel* – this is Yeshua speaking to John the Apostle. It's supremely satisfying.

> *Lift up your mind to comprehend the things I now speak to you. And please share all this with your spiritually endeavoring companions, who, are from the sublime unalterable Race of Humanity.*

> *The One is the supreme Sovereign of all - existing with nothing prior to IT. It is more than a God. The One is the Father of all – the Invisible One that is over all – and who is imperishable – and IS the pure Light .. that no eye can see.*

> *You should not think of The One, as a god; or like a God, with aspects of 'ruling' - because it has no 'Rulership-Lord-Over' associations, within Its loving Self.*

> *The One doesn't exist within any Thing (which would be inferior to It) since everything exists Only within, and By his mind.*

He is Eternal - he does not need anything to be added. The One is absolutely complete; and has never lacked anything, in order to be its sublime completeness.

It has always been, absolutely Whole, in its own Infinite Pure Light.

It is Illimitable; since there is nothing to limit It.

It is unfathomable, since there is nothing that can, or will fathom It.

It is immeasurable, since there is nothing to measure It.

*It is unobservable since nothing Has, or can observe It ..
in Its invisibility.*

*It is Eternal, existing eternally without boundaries or form.
It is Un-utterable since nothing can comprehend it,
or Its being .. to utter.*

*It is un-nameable, since there is nothing above it, to give It a name
It is the immeasurable Light, pure, holy Invisibly Blazing everywhere.*

*It is Perfect .. in Its unutterable Imperishability.
And .. it is not a part of some perfection, (perfectly expressed)
or some blessedness, (sublimely manifest)
nor of some divinity, 'shining'.*

*The One is infinitely Greater and Beyond All of these.
Yet .. It is not measurable.
It is neither corporeal or incorporeal. Neither is It small or large;
It is not expressed so we might say it is 'this much'
... or say, it is 'this type'.*

*No one can understand it ... define It, describe it.
It is not one of the 'things in existence';
It IS EXISTENCE It Self .. and gives it.*

*It is not some Thing to be described, as Greater than.
It is in Itself, its Allness .. and is behind and beyond All ..
as It is not a part of the realm of this expressing, nor of any
sequence of time, or its ephemeral aspects.
For, all that is part of the world (or its expression) was produced by
some other transient aspect producing in a personal activity.*

*Time was never Its field or constraint,
since it receives nothing then .. from any one.*

That is an idea of borrowing. It borrows nothing – needs nothing ..
from any one or any thing.
The Perfect One is inherent Majesty – as Infinite Wholeness, In Itself.

... So what shall I relate to you about the Ineffable Beingness
of The One?

The One is perfect silence. It is at Rest, infinitely As, In, and Being
clarified quietude.

It Conceives of all, as It is before everything .. giving us
ITS conceptions.

It is the Source of all dimensions – emanating and sustaining
Everything anywhere, in Its graceful unending Service and Its
splendorous Generosity.

Yet we would never know about these things – these ineffable
comprehensions - were it not for the fact, that The One sends
messengers to us ..
coming From and speaking Of The One Infinite Father ..
in their sharing with us.

Now the Perfect Complete One beholds Itself, in the Shining Light
that It emanates endlessly (as on the surface of a Spring of Water)
[Consciousness] within, AS, Its many Life forms — living in all the
realms of existence, that IT shines forth into being for experiencing.

It loves its belov'ed reflections on the Surface of this
"reflected conscious Imaging"
"falling in love" with the luminous droplets (its conscious individual
portions) in all of Its infinite consciousness expressing .. and that
surround the Infinite Silent motionless One, endlessly.

Now 'The ForeThought' of The One, became an Idea in Movement,
as a Feminine Creator, congealing and birthing all ideas for
expression (also in the 'Presence' of the Infinite Father).

She is the First Power. She preceded every essence or thing.
She came forth from the Father Mind, as the Fore-Thought of
movement - relating to All and Everything for interaction to occur.

Her Moving Light resembles the Infinite Light of the Father, yet ..
'as a Shining' shedding light all over.

She is the perfect Power. She is the Image of the sublime Breath

of moving Light – transcending, shining, rising, descending,
expanding, contracting .. so that
She is the first Power – the constructing glory of the Womb
of Creativity – and the emerging glorious "Shining forth" ..
of Divine Ideation being made manifest .. ' As' everywhere.

She is praised and glorified in her children as our Pristine Breath,
for She came forth from The One as "Movement and Rest"
everywhere. She is the First Thought and the Moving Image,
in Mind .. Of and In the Breath – Within and Without.

And as the universal Womb, She precedes every thing. She is the
common Parent, in all humanity, as the Holy Breath .. and the
androgynous One in the three names – Father-Mother-Child.

And She is also the eternal realm of motion and rest, for all invisible
and visible beings ..(their resting place) and the realm of purposeful
action, wherein all beings reside to experience all things.

She then asked for the five Eternities of Being.
And The One agreed.   She asked for:

Forethought, Foreknowledge, Life Eternal, Truth and Imperishability

She received them.

The One entered into Her Moving-Resting Lovethought-Being -
projecting forth a Ray, as each of us, not as bright as Her,
but each Child of us, was a union of The One and the Mother -
- the infinite conscious One in stillness; and the omnipresent Breath-
of movement and activity - in inter-active Beingness.

~ Yeshua Christ ~ (adapted from Marvin Meyer's translation)

THE ORIGINAL MESSAGE

Let us here go deeply into the philosophical underpinnings, causes,
historical and spiritual inertia of Yeshua' world.   He came to us delivering a message to heal and empower the human psyche no matter our
country for each person individually.

He taught how to live in a divine kingdom within.. while living our
Earth life. ' The kingdom of God is within us' he said. We may be in the
world without being of it.

This kingdom is a subjective reality, and a personal life-experience.

To put it simply, Christ came to heal the 'separated' Human Psyche, by revealing *how to breach the barrier between our Elevated Divine consciousness* and our human awareness in showing and practicing the God experience.

When honoring Yeshua' teachings, a renovation occurs in our personal awareness, which yields a truly spiritual inner Light, transforming the way we See and the way we live our life – the way we Feel about our self. Then we feel the *God Experience* daily by following Yeshua private spiritual teachings.

His private teaching to his disciples with its discipline (revealed herein) and in *Thomas' Gospel*, is the source of the Spiritual authority in life. Christ taught it then and brought it to us here as well - in his revelation on Experiential Spirituality.

The New Covenant with God was unveiled by Yeshua in his mission and ministry, in the four biblical gospels and in Thomas where his beautiful instructions are given in elegant simplicity. Absorbing it we experience the true Path within, and we discover Christ's transformative secrets-revealing *how to rise into our True power* .. surrendering to superior Truth, and a superior Self-Awareness .. in The God Experience.

This, is Christ's unparalleled offering of power, from his unparalleled teaching. Friends, welcome to the Original Message.

~ PROLOGUE ~

WHY THOMAS NOW?
MIGHT ITS DISCOVERY HAVE BEEN GUIDED?

Friends, this book arose from a constant compelling urge to write. Thomas for me is like having a twin brother: *same DNA* - different life experience. My mentor, William Samuel, handed me this gospel in February 1990, and I was instantly taken with it. William had "schooled" me through the auspices of his own books in that which lies beyond religion.

He introduced this former ministerial student and preacher to a world of pure awareness - to its *source and sublime interior process* to unfetter conscious awareness from the three-dimensional thinking of ego. William's books and The Gospel of Thomas reveal a way to relax into The God Experience to realize and experience Divine Being in our very consciousness and breath.

This was the ancient Secret if you were wondering. *Consciousness and Breath* ARE the Divine Presence in our Life. Do we wish to know how close God is to us? Can it be closer than consciousness and breathing? No. That's as close as it gets.

The body is the vehicle for our Earth experience, but our IDENTITY (*That IS who we are forever)* is our Consciousness and Breath. The body is the Vehicle-car. We are the driver. Consciousness is the omnipresent motionless infinite deific Mind in you and me and all life, (actually everywhere) experiencing every moment of existence omnipresently. You need someone at the very foundation to plan, initiate, and guide all activities in the Universe. Thank you Father. Now Breath is the Etheric moving portion of God - animating every particle of time-space, every cell and corpuscle of our blood stream, in life force energy. It's The Message of ancient scriptures. Consciousness is the Father - Breath the Mother.

In the words of Christ to his disciples, recorded in this ancient gospel, he pointed the way to a personal *relationship-experience* with our inner

Divine Essence (Consciousness and Breath) which projects our earthly human appearance; even while we seem so human (in our bodies). To give a slightly deeper frame of reference, we might think of the Divine breath as our Feminine divine aspect, and our Divine Consciousness as the masculine aspect. The consciousness conceives and the moving constructing Breath, manifests; Consciousness *plans* - Breath *constructs*. As Kahlil Gibran says in his masterpiece, 'the Prophet'...

> " *Is it not your breath that has hardened and erected*
>   *the structure of your bones...*
>
> *And is it not a Dream which none of you remember having dreamt,*
> *that builded your city and fashioned all there is In it.*"

ONENESS

Many have heard the Idea that we are one with God, but we wonder just *how does this oneness look?* Where is this oneness anyway? How does it show up? Why does the Apostle Paul say that *We are the Temple of God... that God lives within us and walks and talks in us?* It is your Consciousness and your Breath. This means that the Divine is in and As each moment. Get ready now to be completely *shocked - amazed*. Listen. *Spirit* is the Latin word for *Breath*. With that information, you'll plainly SEE that the Bible is all about *Breath* and *soul-Consciousness*. Had the translators not used the *Latin word* for breath, in place of the English word BREATH, we would have seen this for 400 years, but they did not do so properly.

  For this primary reason the biblical books have been misunderstood for centuries, because a foreign word (*that no one Knew Meant Breath- Breathe*) was inserted into an English document-version. How would you like it if someone inserted a Zulu or Swahili word in your wedding vows, your favorite poem or song, and you never knew it was even foreign, or that it meant something quite common to you, yet you did not know it. It was just a weird word. And you thought it had a different meaning altogether.

  Pneuma is Greek for breath and breathe. It has *5 meanings* in Greek - *breathe, breath, blast of breath, current of breath & Wind*. Its Root **Pneo** means **Breathe Hard.** Why would English translators (*paid to translate to English*) use a *Latin word* for Breath? Yeshua said to the Samaritan women at the well, in John 4:23-24 *"GOD IS BREATH, and they that worship God, must truly worship him in their breath.*

Not very fair for those biblical translators, To Be PAID to translate from Greek to English, is it, and then .. on the most powerful Meaningful word in the scripture, **make a stop at Latin**, and insert a *Latin word instead is it?* Oh My Word! This is the quintessential '*Lost In Translation.*' (It was not the assignment at all, to confuse us -- WAS IT)?

Spirit is even indeed found in the middle of words like *re-Spiration, re-Spirate,* in a hospital *re-Spirator, ex-Spire (breathe out a last breath or Die)* **in-Spire** (*to inward breathe from divine inspiration*). Yet No one knows it means to Breathe or Breath – but go to a dictionary, even a *Latin dictionary* and it's right there. You will be shocked that someone, has put over on the rest of us an obfuscation of the true scriptural instructions for how to live stratospherically and peacefully in our Earth experience. Once we know we connect in *purifying contact* with divine etheric essence and god's frequency lifting substance, *in a Conscious breath, we transform life.*

It was Paul who taught the Fruits of The Holy Breath and brought their description out in 1 Corinthians 13. *Haggion Pneuma* is the Greek for the Holy or Sacred Breath (*which the translators inserted as the Latin word SPIRIT instead of the English word Breath*). Why use a Latin word?

Yeshua Breathed with them, saying: Receive you the Holy 'Pneuma, breath, [spirit]. John 20:22. Can you see it? Yeshua BREATHED with them; not ON them, with them. He taught it right there. The Greek preposition is translated **With** *in grammar rules.* No Spiritual Teacher-leader ever gave more, to so many, or was more generous. We wouldn't know this by the translator's work. Yeshua Christ and John the Baptist had planned to introduce the Essene water baptism first, after which Yeshua would introduce the Breath Of Light, or Fire. They had their plan well organized.

THE FIRE EXPERIENCE OF THE BREATH — THE SECRET OF THE AGES

Remember this in the Matthew 3:11, when John the Baptist said:

"*I baptize with water only, but he that comes after me ...*

shall baptize with the Holy [Pneuma] Breath (spirit)... and Fire".

John did not himself baptize people in the Sacred Breath; he submerged them in water, as an Essene elder would. When folks got out of the water, they were wet and had to dry off. Yeshua was teaching something different. What he brought in his powerful Breath teaching created Fire and Heat for the newly baptized individual. It was different from being wet and chilled. *What is this Fire John mentioned?* It is a cleansing, healing, transformative secret come to us from Yeshua' generosity. No one else dared. Religion had kept it from the masses. Realize, the Breath discipline was the second-stage-Essene-discipline (after a water baptism). It was what each Essene practiced daily ... their entire life.

You should also know that this spiritual breath technology is in harmony with the teaching on yoga-breath which is almost entirely about the breathing. A full seventy per cent of Yoga is in the breath. Many think it is mostly physical dance movements. They are in the smaller percentage. As said earlier, this knowledge of the breath is ancient and widespread amongst the truly privileged – disciples, royalty, and serious-minded wealthy. Yeshua gave the most powerful knowledge so that everyone in the world could have it. Friends, did that get through? Yeshua gave it to EVERYONE. Yet it's what was hidden for 2000 more years.

Know this fact: A fiery heat occurs in our body when we are breathing powerfully for an extended time during spiritual exercises. Here is the secret: *This Breath can transform our body and consciousness from one phase-state to another. Like water can become a vapor, and caterpillars become butterflies, the heat generated during this Breathing, can phase us into a light-body frequency. We are still the same molecular composition, yes but our state of being rises into new frequency harmonics.* Our body begins taking on a higher vibrational reality. It has Heat, light and Higher States in it.

With the lengthy presence of deeply inhaled oxygen (a necessary element in all fires) and which we breathe in deeply during the Holy Breathing exercise, the spark of electricity in every cell of our body-electric flares up (in 100 trillion cells). Without oxygen fires go out; with it they flame up. Even in the movie *The Ten Commandments*, when the Pillar of Fire blocks Yul Brynner's chariot, his lieutenant calls it the "Breath of God". The Fire element is always known this way.

We have heard the phrase "purifying fire" for millennia. Fire is used to purify *everything- gold, precious metals too*. Why wouldn't the presence of oxygen in our body from this Breathing In, fire up the flame of purification in our physical electrical body (temple) even, and especially in our brain cells? Firsthand experience let's one know that our brain cells feel, not only wonderful, but so elevated and enthralled with the experience of this discipline, that we cannot imagine, ever giving up, the blessing of it.

As mentioned there is a heat that's experienced when breathing purposefully for extended periods of time. This awareness comes from personal experience where we can find ourselves and our chair or carpet, where seated, completely soaked in a pool of our own perspiration with rosy skin tone. Runners know this exquisite enlivening heat when they enter the Zone during a workout—when they are breathing deeply. However, this is not about exercise, but a conscious choice to worship breathing. This is done in private, with God, not on a tennis court.

This Heat and its transformative action in our body cleanses and heals the body from within. This powerful secret to human health promotes such purification that we can be in excellent health in an ongoing way. Germs and viruses do not find a conducive environment to live in the body .. because the Heat from the deep breath drives them out.

This Deep Breath exercise can be used to burn out colds, flu, asthma, even cancer and addictions, *particularly smoking* which actually decreases the benefit of the Holy Breath within our lungs by clogging them up, reducing their effectiveness significantly. By practicing this new spiritual technology, we can burn out the tar and nicotine, as well as other impurities such as heavy metals, smog, pesticides etc., as well as any proclivity to cancer that could be there waiting to rise up.

Nobel Laureate Dr. Otto Warberg showed that cancer cells cannot live in a healthy alkaline environment in the human body. The opposite— *acidity*—arises from diets of sweets, alcohol, coffee, soft drinks, sugars, smoking, processed flour, and processed foods. Cancer thrives on these. The Heat generated during the Breathing exercise burns sugars and acids right out of our system, by atomizing them back into free-form energy.

Once we GET that by *Breathing in* the etheric moving portion of infinite formless Divine Being, we will raise our body's and our Mind's frequency, we will see why it was being taught by Christ and apostle Paul. Doing so provides spiritual gifts and true tangible upliftment to us.

We are down here on an Earth visit, to feel salient and rich, *amazingly deep experiences,* and we CAN enjoy this in power and grace but not if we don't know the truth of our very being - how to access it, feel it, luxuriate in it, learn from it, and be blessed and empowered by it. So what do we do? **Listen to Yeshua.** The answers have been there for two millennia.

SPIRITUALITY IS DAY BY DAY

It's a step-by-step process that God enjoys in each one of us as we rediscover our Source, our Oneness and Identity, as and with Divine Consciousness. and the infinite breath. The blissful journey back to Divine Awareness is what we're all doing here on Earth. William Samuel's writing helps release metaphysics from old forms of religiosity. He not only quoted Thomas in his own books as a source of inspiration and teaching, but he placed it in my hand, suggesting its perusal. Focusing on Thomas changed my life. I studied the book with great passion and dedication, and it lifted my outlook and spiritual attunement.

I also spent inspired time with William and his wife Rachel (who are now passed) at their home in Mountain Brook, Alabama. I got to sleep in his beloved Wood Song bungalow, where he did all his famous writings over the decades. One day while looking at photos on his mantle, I spied a family name and William and I realized we were kin. We formed a deeper bond of mind and sharing from that, which I will always treasure.

I then submerged myself in Thomas for nine years, up to and just past the millennium celebration. I was in Hong Kong at the completion of interpreting Thomas. There was a special feeling being in Hong Kong. My time in the orient was a spiritual landmark in my life. After nine years in a creative process, one feels a very special satisfaction.

One night in meditation in my hotel room, a downloading of the *Mystic Traveler* film story came to me (perhaps its words as well). It occurred over a quarter-hour. It seemed limitless rectangular images flew by me like Movie-Screens going past my vision at light-speed. It was an awesome powerful experience.

Now, The Gospel of Thomas is said by some to have been given to the disciples just after Yeshua' resurrection, during private lectures in the seven weeks before his departure on the Jewish holy day, Pentecost. All other New Testament books were written fifteen to seventy-five years later after this holy day. See for yourself, how similar the Thomas Gospel is to the others. So many quotes in it are similar to theirs, that it's easy to see why they thought of his material being 'sourse.' Thomas opens very uniquely,

"These are the Secret Words spoken by the Living Yeshua... and recorded ... by Didymus Judas Thomas."

Yeshua begins:

> *Those who discover the significance of these words*
> *shall not Taste death.*
>
> *Let those who seek, not cease from their seeking until they Find.*
>
> *When they find, they will be troubled, and after this, will be in*
> *Wonder. Then, they will reign over The All.*

Now, for the first time there exists an interpretation of Thomas for the modern mind. Its esoteric, poetic code-language is finally explicated and amplified in clarity, placing it into the language of spiritual discernment.

The Bible reveals that Yeshua often spoke in parables, metaphor and symbolic images, so his disciples would understand him but no one else. Yeshua said many times, "Now here is the meaning." The Bible and Thomas are both written in this secretive symbolic imagery.

By producing an interpretive explication of the Thomas Gospel, found in 1945, its metaphorical mystical message can be plainly understood. Its carbon dating is right in line with all the other gospel manuscripts, essentially the same age.

This book was not written to enter debates (scholars often debate). It was written to inspire seekers with the essence of the matter. At the heart of anything is its essence. There are many aspects on the periphery of any matter, but when we wash away the external, diverting, superfluous, distracting aspects, we find the heart of the thing. For example, take away all peripheral aspects of a human life. What is left? *Breath, Sense Consciousness, Love and Body-Life-Force.* The essence of scriptural meaning is similar.

In relation to the 1st and 2nd-century documents like Thomas (*or any New Testament book)* the essence of its instruction is key. Our heart must arrive at its principles to experience and know them. *Without* a focus on essence, scholars often argue about lesser aspects - cities, regions, dates potential writers' names, etc. - but, for us, our heart reveals its essence. Our heart reveals the key.

You see, we can't say with certainty who wrote any biblical book because we weren't there to observe the writing from thousands years ago. We simply surmise or come to believe who authored them. Even though books such as Matthew and Luke have those names ascribed to them, since we were not there to watch them write, we cannot say who actually wrote them, because they were written decades later. So to gain true understanding, we study, ponder, assimilate, review, correlate its principles, *then our heart reveals the essence of its meaning* to our mind.

This interpretation of Thomas was inspired by a nine-year, long-lived honoring of heart and soul. It is based on inner spiritual experience in consciousness and breath, and the awareness of the esoteric Interpretative Method which is rarely applied, to scripture these days. The Bible's code-language and esoteric way of looking is essentially not considered by many people. Many scholars wish to interpret and explicate in literal ways—but Christ taught in metaphor and symbol.

The historical, political and literal manner of explanation is unfortunately used by too many. Yet Yeshua and Paul used the inner esoteric method of explanation and instruction. Yeshua' esoteric way of teaching is ever present in his gospel instruction. Why don't scholars see this? I have wondered. Why don't they realize that their literal method doesn't work so well with parable, metaphor and allegory? They can't leave literal ways 'behind'.

Even TV programs covering biblical topics on the History Channel or Discovery Channel seem to present only the old-time Exoteric view. It's like preschool. Informed folks just shake their head. You see the TV writers they hire, have no knowledge of the inner way of understanding spiritual material. So their TV scripts deliver old time religion to the unsuspecting masses. My interpretation of the book of Revelation is very 'Different'. Old-time views on that book are 'literal'. You will see the difference between these two forms here in this book, in the code language in Thomas's interpretation. So this book's presentation will unfold the differences in the meanings. It will be illuminating.

If we're desiring to become familiar with the inner and deeper way of understanding spiritual material, we've come to the right place. We will find this spirituality is more about our heart and soul, our mind and breath, than religious rituals and ceremonies. This way of understanding spiritual material is fulfilling to our most interior beingness, our real Self. When we realize that we are not beings made of meat, we have come halfway home. Our breath and consciousness become the pathway to understanding and realizing our eternal Identity.

THE POWER OF PARABLE, METAPHOR AND ALLEGORY

Making the *Literal* worse, ancient scriptures are written in symbolic words -and for a wise and insightful reason. Words mean different things to each of us within even one language, let alone many languages throughout history. Communicating with words has uncertainty attached. Ask many people what they just heard and we get many different understandings.

Facilitating a *code-language* with agreed-to conceptual images was a brilliant idea. Instead of words we utilize concepts and imagery. Using metaphor, allegory and parable in spiritual communication is like a currency we pass between us to communicate with pre-understood nuances; as in, *"a picture is worth a thousand words."*

So let's make 'Meekness' into a picture. Meekness means *guidability, leadability, teachability, deference, perhaps a highly developed spiritual nature.* I just used a few words to describe Meekness. It could be hundreds. Here's what the ancient writers did: *lamb* was a common word-picture to represent *Meekness/Spirituality;* (*lion* meant *ego*) so whenever they wrote or read lamb in the text they knew it's inner meaning; (*sheep-shepherd* were also related to this lamb/meekness topic in the spiritual code). *Bird* means *'intuition'. Water*=*mind; fire*= *breath-purification*; *Light*= *awareness; Tree*= *spiritual life path*; *Bush*= *body of instruction.* There are so many.

See, using left-brain language to inspire Meekness in readers, the lesson words could be misunderstood - because words can have a morass of different meanings, depending on one's background. It would end up like that game from childhood where, in a line, one whispers a message to the next and, by the end of the line the message comes out fully different.

Where, how, and who created the symbolic way of communicating is not known. Maybe it was God. It is as old as storytelling, particularly in written form. Both the Bible and the Thomas Gospel were written in this code-language, which is why we may hear that the spiritual material confuses us. Very often, to many modern readers, reading scripture is like reading the headlines of a newspaper without getting the articles that go with the headlines. Many of us don't have insight into the meanings of scriptural statements, without some explanation. Many people have a little incredulity when they read scripture. *They just don't get it – the meaning doesn't sink in.* To avoid this frustration, many people don't read scriptural material at all.

SPIRITUAL CODE

The modern interpretation herein helps readers of Thomas by revealing the meaning of the spiritual code in it. This new expanded version uses modern words and ideas, drawing on many sources to explicate the gospel's meaning in its metaphysical instruction.

As a student of many ancient scriptures, including the New Testament, in this interpretive treatise I've used freeform paraphrasing to elucidate Thomas's inner meaning. This treatise therefore is not a translation – there are already many of those. This interpretation of Thomas is an amplifying unfoldment, of ancient symbolism, which can be challenging to understand in the older words.

In explicating the code-language of ancient texts with modern words and ideas we *reveal the secrets behind the symbolic words*. Also in interpreting the code words, we replaced words like *spirit with breath* because Spirit simply means *breath or breathe* in Latin. Ergo, this document is not an exact word-for-word exposition. *We have many already.. that sound alike.*

Rather, this interpretation is meant to open up the mystical instruction in each verse of Thomas; *which it does with illustrative paraphrasing and prose,* as well as analogies and quotations from the Bible, Kahlil Gibran, Lao Tzu and many famous spiritual masters. Incidentally, Mystical means the *knowledge of and the pursuit of conscious union with Divine Being.* By this we understand that prayer and meditation are mystical activities. So these verses from a few thousand years ago are interpreted here for your benefit. The 114 verses are each brief, so I expanded them for clarity.

I also perceived another peculiar thing providing an added mystery. I noticed many passages seemed to be randomly inserted in the text with no real order (as if compiled quickly or thrown together hastily); as if someone made a hasty uninformed copy. Some of the verses appear to be in a proper order, while too many others are unrelated in subject matter to the surrounding text. Still others, answer a question posed pages earlier.

One can just imagine how ordinary real-world concerns or troublesome matters might have influenced either the transcribing or collation of the thoughts in the scrolls. It may be that what we found in in the earthenware jar is a copy of a once more complete set of scroll-works, in a different order than in this one. I believe it was much larger, back then. The bedouin who found it claimed several scrolls were burned for kindling.

So to point out a few examples one can easily see that logia 14 answers the question in the first half of logia 6 (*not the second half of 6*); and verse 13 does not ask a question that 14 answers. Another example is logia 92 (which has important spiritual implications in it) is not appropriately served or *related* to verse 93; nor does 93 logically follow the subject in 92. So in this Interpretation of Thomas, verse 6 is split in half (the logical thing to do) with 14 answering. The salient message in verse 27 now answers 92 because it seemed the most appropriate verse in the book to follow such a spiritually portentous statement.

These are just a few examples; there are many adjustments in order. Anyone with an eye for Thought-Progression can see that the content from one verse to another is not related to or served by its neighboring verse. Most of the verses are now re-arranged in our interpretation to reveal their meaning providing a flowing continuity of ideas, in spiritual principles which builds structure. Verses are now next to verses related in subject and/or tone, flowing together nicely from one idea to the next.

So, where 'Thomas' was done in the code-imagery of ancient words – in no real order - it is now presented with coherent ideas, in a natural continuity. Because we've *translated the Code here,* it now enjoys modern-word clarity. It becomes relevant to people of our day, with our comprehension. This presentation is placed in eleven chapters that lead us through the passages or phases we may face on our spiritual path. This was written for 21st century Minds - for the *way We* read

'WORD FOR WORD' FOR SO MANY DECADES NOW

Thomas has been translated word-for-word over several decades since 1945, by many authors who did not understand the code-language of spiritual metaphor (*which is why they translated the words only but not the symbolism*). When read, their versions sound so similar we wonder why so many? This explicated interpretation of Thomas is completely different and has never before been attempted.

It's exciting that a gospel scroll remained untouched, hidden in sand, for the better part of two millennia. The fact that it wasn't edited by anyone in a religious setting testifies to its purity. The idea that we may read a spiritual message from nearly 2000 years ago, knowing it was not affected by anyone's agenda, provides a feeling of portent. This purity makes the Gospel's assimilation exciting.

Some say, why would a Divine Agency save an ancient scroll untouched for a few millennia? *We say, why Not?* It makes sense that the Divine would preserve one gospel record purely from long ago so we could enjoy its true essence. Perhaps the best was saved for last.

It is well known that Thomas actually did travel to Egypt and then, India. To this day there is a 'Church of Thomas' in India. So discovering in Egyptian sand Yeshua' brother's gospel of Thomas has already been the inspiration for several exciting movie-thrillers over many decades. If Hollywood produces a story repeatedly over 50 years, it must be good.

The Gospel of Thomas has all the mystery wisdom one would expect a Master to give his disciples. It's not a storytelling gospel—it's just 114 quotations. Why would Yeshua tell his life story to his disciples just after they already lived it with him? He would simply speak, teach, lecture, conveying statements or principles before departing.

The words and statements in the Thomas Gospel were meant to inspire, instruct, and uplift Yeshua' listeners with transformational lessons, while someone like a brother inscribed his words.

This document was plainly meant for our Age. It comes from a few thousand years ago unaltered. We may see from it Yeshua' private teachings and thinking.

May I suggest reading this in its order, which is building stone upon stone and is crucial for truly connecting with and understanding its metaphorical and mystical wisdom. Thomas' scroll is an inspiring source of transformational instruction; from Yeshua' lips to Thomas's papyrus, and finally, to our Hearts.

A SAMPLE OF ESSENE SPIRITUAL MATERIAL

Adapted from: *Praising God At All Times*, Column Ten, from "The Manuel of Discipline" found at the Essene Library in Qumran, Israel (the Dead Sea Scrolls).

> *As long as I live, it shall be a rule engraved on my tongue to bring Praise, like fruit for an offering—and my lips shall be a Sacrificial Gift. I will make skillful music with lyre and harp to serve God's glory, and the flute of my lips I shall raise in Praise regarding His*

Rule of Righteousness. Both morning and evening I shall enter into this Covenant with God: and at the end of both, I shall recite His commands, and so long as they exist ... there will be my frontier, and there, my journey's end.

Therefore I will bless His Divine name [I Am] in all I do and say; And before I move hand or foot, and whenever I go Out or come In; or whenever I sit down, and whenever I rise up, and even when lying on my couch, I will chant God's Praise.

*My lips shall praise **He Who Is** as I sit at the table, which is set for all, and before I lift my hands to partake of any nourishment, from the delicious fruits of the earth, I will perform this personal love.*

*And even when fear or terror come, and there is only anguish and distress, I will bless and thank **He Who Is** for the wondrous deeds of His creation story; and I will meditate upon Her power, and lean upon His mercies all day long.*

For in His hand is Justice for all who live, and all Her works are true. So, when either trouble comes, or salvation, I will praise God, just the same.

Finally.. The God Experience, to which our book is dedicated, transcends our human awareness and lifts us to such higher levels, we begin to See and feel into the truth of our Identity - and our true place in the universe. This fleshly home we live in - inside the universe - begins to reveal and unfold its secrets to us by attending to The God Experience inside our Being.

The One daily unfolds our awesome relation to Divine Life, and to the spiritual and physical universes both. Realizing this, we know what to look for, in reading and assimilating the material from these remarkable and ancient documents.

Near the end of the book we will reveal what *Yeshua meant,* as Being Baptized (immersed) in the Holy Breath (pneuma - spirit).

DIVINE WORDS and IDEAS - MADE INTO FLESH

In the beginning was The WORD-Idea   [I]
and The WORD-Idea was with God   [I AM]
and The WORD-Idea Was God.   [I AM the I AM]
          [in All this]
All things *were made* by The WORD-Idea [I AM *That* I AM]
and outside of this *WORD-Idea Expression* is not anything made.

In Him [*in the expression of the Divine Word-Idea*] is Life,
and this life is the Light in all of humankind.

This is the true light of Divine Being,
which lights every soul that comes into the world.

Adapted from John 1:1, 3-4, 9

"These are secret teachings of the Living Yeshua …"
~ Recorded by Didymus Judas Thomas~

A note on the typesetting in this modern interpretations: All Caps words and-or **Bold** *can indicate a word maybe a* **Code Word**--*one of the Secret symbolic words that need amplification and interpretation. Such words typically will have an explanation immediately following them, in parentheses, to illustrate their inner significance.*

You'll also notice that the Interpretation of Thomas uses the line-length and spacing of poetry. This visible treatment of the dialogue between the Master and his disciples simply provides a visual setting that lends itself to an ease of assimilation. Enjoy.

I

THE DECISION:
TO JOURNEY BACK TO THE LIGHT

Yeshua began speaking to his disciples,
and looking into their eyes, he spoke powerfully to them:
If you discern the significance behind my words,
you will not make transition from life through 'Death'
[through a state of transitional non-awareness]. 1.

If you are truly a spiritual seeker, you must seek within your deep Self—
inside your Consciousness and Breath—your True Identity;
Touching these realms you may find your original I AM Awareness
deep within you; for these are your connection Point to Divine Being ...
and they are *in you*. Finding Your center, your life will soar gracefully.
So do not cease from your spiritual seeking until you find your
I AM Center; for you will be tempted to give up your spiritual pursuit
before you find it, and you will be troubled before you find your bliss.
But do not fear over difficulties.
It is simple, if you seek enthusiastically like a child.
And when you arrive in your Deep Self,
you will be awed and in wonder,
— seeing your oneness with The All — and after being in wonder
you will reign over The All [over universal manifestation]. 2.

If like some, you pursue earthly knowledge, to know "The All"
[the Universe] but yet, if you do not yet know the depths of your own Self,
you have missed everything. For the Self and The All are One ... but the
Self is here within us, and it is to be deeply felt, and it is where *Bliss* is
realized. The Self and The All are the "within and without" of each other.
But the *Invisible Divine Self* in us, is greater; it *expresses* that which is visible.
The deep Self is our home.
It is our Origin, and our Destination, in spiritual pursuits. 67.

I shall give you what no eye has seen, nor ear heard,
nor hand touched, nor any heart received.
What I give you now are the Mysteries of Being,
for which true seekers hunger and thirst. 17.

I will lead my brothers and sisters into their Blissful Being,
one from a thousand, and two from ten thousand—yet each
shall arrive at bliss in his own time;
and no matter where they each are, they shall all eventually stand united
within this wondrous and expansive Consciousness. 23.

These secrets are revealed to those who treasure them.
Do not treat them lightly.
Do not boast spiritually, talking endlessly to others about your spiritual life.
Keep your inner spirituality as a treasure unto yourself.
Place the "coal of fire" upon your lips.
Do not let your **Left Hand** [your outer life] know.. what your
Right Hand [your inner spiritual activity] is doing.
Do not spend your enthusiasm for your spiritual path in idle talk.
Do not use up your dedication for this New Mind in ego chatter.

For he who controls his tongue "can take a CITY"
[can enter a new state of consciousness]. 62.

One who is seeking within shall find Me,
and doors will be opened to one who knocks looking for Me. 94.

If you seek for your Origin within your own consciousness,
you shall discover that the Infinite I AM is truly your own Presence.
And then your moment-to-moment life purpose
can be continuously revealed to you.

This guidance will activate your transformation out of ego constraints
and it will engender spiritual creativity.
This creativity, when operating in concert with Divine Initiative,
will create True Self expression, and the unfoldment of your divine destiny.
I was asked something recently, and I did not answer you then, but I want
to tell you now the *secret of transformation* that you asked about earlier. 92.

Unless you *Abstain* from the world and its ego-driven pursuits,
you will not find the quiet, yet expansive awareness in your Center.
Unless you honor and live the Sabbath Rest in everyday life—
resting from fearful worry, worldly lusts and the pursuit of "things"—
you will not see your Divine Soul as your living cause;
nor will you see your Holy Breath as it is — a Nurturing Expandingness.

Both Soul and Breath, work In you As you to create True Self awareness.
Soul-*Consciousness* ... is the Divine Father Life within.
Spirit-*Breath* is the Divine Mother – a moving constructive life force
within. *Meditation* makes us one-with the Mind of Father God.
Divine Breath work makes us into *Divine beings* on Earth in true awareness.
This pure awareness will take dominion over your "appetites,"
instead of your appetites taking dominion over you.
Performing *daily* the simple sacred acts of Love with your Inner, does it.

This activity will transform the Entirety of your life experience. 27.

When Spiritual Messengers visit you, and give to you your Truth
[the truth of your inner being],
for your part give them your full attention
and give them the substance of your now-moment awareness.

After they have given you their gift, learn from them
the source of their power, which is their dedication of purpose
to unify Heaven and Earth for you and for everyone. 88.

Otherwise, why have you chosen to enter The Service of Divine Being?
Was it to see the things of Earth tremble with spiritual power?
Or to excitedly watch your earthly form quiver and transform under the
influence of spiritual experiences, *like dazedly watching some magician's act?*
Are you in it to see "signs and wonders," or are you here to help others?

Did you come onto the Path to increase your material goods and wealth
and are you wanting to acquire and wear fine clothes and jewelry?
Your kings and queens and wealthy people all wear fine clothing, yet they
do not see the truth of our divine Identity.

If you are seeking fine clothing, you will not be able to find the door to the **Kingdom** [God's true domicile within your consciousness] for it requires your sincerity and your exuberance ... and your enthusiasm.
You cannot deceive your Spiritual Self.

Seek without and you can get the things of the world from the world.
Seek within and you will find your Eternal Beingness. 78.

The ministers, bishops and priests of churchianity receive opportunities to learn the keys of understanding true spirituality in their religious studies; but they seek not the real treasure.

And like the blind leading the blind, religious institutions do not teach them the truth of within-ness, and these ministers do not ferret out the keys to use them or teach them.

So the keys are hidden from the people as well, to whom they preach.
And by living and teaching about outer things these ministers hinder the people with ceremonies and rituals and things — *that entertain the mind*;
They ask for money, allegiance, and penance to themselves; and in empty words lift themselves up, while they hide the Divine One within each one of us. They do not lead you to the "I AM I" of your Deep Self,
but keep you down in the realm of rituals and guilt.

These religious systems mostly glorify human egos, and they subordinate one person to another person, or to an organization; which have no authority or capacity to confer justification, forgiveness, or righteousness, upon you or anyone.

That blessing comes from within you, not from without you.
But I say: The hour is coming and now is when the true worshippers shall truly worship their divine I AM in spirituality [in privacy and creativity] —in meditation and inner inspiration—(in the Deep Conscious Breath) which is the Holy Spirit's now-moment embrace.
This experiential worship unifies you with divinity:
the earthly with the heavenly, and the body with the holy Breath.

And we shall worship our I AM in true centeredness from that Fiery place within... and from our Light Being, [mingling personality awareness with that divine etheric expression] - where Consciousness merges with breathing, and Awareness with loving.

For the heavenly I AM is seeking for us to love and worship in this way, as this form of love and worship expands the "I" back into the I AM and this love reveals the Infinite in the individual. [J]

Graceful expressions of love and power will come into the world through the Visible One and yet from the invisible Infinite One.
But most ministers do not enter this Expansive Consciousness within, remaining instead in their earthly persona,
where they can exercise their control over people.
They will not allow heavenly entrance
to those who wish to meet our Father Mother God,
for they themselves would be left behind.

Therefore, be wise as serpents and innocent as doves;
Take into your own hands
The Search for entering the Expansive Awareness of your own being.

Only you can experience your own bliss
and it is only in your own being that you experience God. 39.

Troubles shall come to false teachers. They are like a dog in a cattle barn.
The dog will not eat oats, but he will not allow the oxen to eat it either;
and this contentiousness shall come back against him,
[as a swift kick from somewhere]. 102.

First learn this: Our Divine Selfhood has three aspects
and it exists within each of two worlds.
Each of us is a part of two dualistic worlds:
the world of our *creative consciousness* - inside us
and the world of effect, of *physical matter,* of that which appears as out here.
These two worlds are one, but consciousness actually gives birth
to the world of effect.

It's our invisible essence, our Creative Consciousness and our Spirit breath
which creates our visible circumstances, and the world in which we live.
Unfortunately, most on earth share a limiting or a fearful self-image
in consciousness. The violence, selfishness and domineering systems
of this world, inculturate earthly minds in a negative and tentative manner.
It is these poor ideas in consciousness .. our ego-self-image, and *our*
attitudes, that manifest our personal and collective experience here
on the earth plane.

We sometimes may appear to be lost in our visible circumstances,
but we are only ignoring the Invisible Power of our personal consciousness
which is our *heavenly* Aspect ... and is our divinely creative Essence.
In our permanent heavenly state of being, in our deep Self, our Self has
three aspects and each aspect serves its own purpose in our life.
Our three-sided essence includes: our *Soul, our Breath, and our Body*
as three parts of one being. These three-in-one work as one to create
each moment of our life experience.
Learn the purpose of each, and take dominion over non-conscious creation
in your life. Non-conscious creation is our trap. For we are learning
to be conscious creators — creating from love — in Awareness.

Here is the understanding of our three aspects. Let us first look at our Soul.
Our SOUL is like a father.
Our soul is actually a part of and one-with Infinite Divine Being.
Our soul is our Source of consciousness and .. is present everywhere.

Our soul conveys to our awareness our supra-conscious **"I"**.

Our soul is the starting place of love in us, our pure desires and true initiative.
It conveys our living Will into our life, creating our focused Attention,
and it is the Source of our loving radiance, which we shine upon
our loved ones, and upon our interests and desires.

Like a captain, our Soul guides our divine destiny, even when we don't
know it; and if we listen to its guidance, our Soul leads us gracefully ..
in each moment.
Now, our BREATH-Spirit is like a mother.

Like a womb, our own spirit creates and nurtures what we hold consistently in the consciousness of our soul.
With each breath, our spirit projects our "subjective awareness" directly into our lives; By manifesting that personal vision of life that we continuously hold in our subconscious or conscious mind.

Our BREATH manifests our inner "**I AM**".

Our BREATH-spirit is the secret *Intelligence* united *with-In* our consciousness creating our subconscious vision and plans in magical detail. How, we know not, but it does.
Through the activity of our spirit, we visibly see what we really feel about our self and our life.

In each breath, our spirit gathers Cosmic Substance to form our deeply held beliefs, manifesting them here. Also, our spirit produces these strongest visions and desires, whether they are positive or negative.

Our spirit is an infinite Secret Force working invisibly everywhere to out-picture our innermost world, and our self-image. This is why we need to actually groom our subconscious self-image, in inner time and creativity. So, it is our Spirit that faithfully and mysteriously produces our most insistent motivations in consciousness. Our spirit works for us in every breath breathed — twenty four hours a day.

Now, our BODY – like a child – is an expression of our *Father-Mind-Soul* and *Mother-BREATH-spirit*. Our body is a "form" in light substance projected by our soul's desire and our spirit's creativity.

Our body is our conscious and visibly formed "**I**".

So, our body is a visible expression in form of our innermost self conception. It is a visible "I" expressed from our invisible ideas of "I AM this and that." Like a mirror, our earthly body reflects our strongest identifications and our deeply felt self–images, which we continually hold inside of us.

But realize this: Our earthly body is really more an image of our former beliefs, and our past self-images that are still visible now.

In our "heavenly state" our soul, spirit, and light body are the
"three-in-one" operating in the now to effect some creation momentarily.
They constantly create. It is their purpose.

That which is visible now as your life, is a picture of *past* beliefs.
To improve our life we must therefore take our focus off of appearances
— off of the current situation — which depicts our past, and go within
to create anew, instead — *from our Invisible Creative Consciousness.*
If we do not go within to create anew, our past decisions continue.

Our soul, spirit and body represent our *wholeness in unification,* in the now.

They are c*onsciousness, creative intelligence,* and *expressiveness* in visible form.
However, in our earthly awareness these are not always consciously unified.
And this is because our ego's reactive mentation is constantly evaluating
and judging everything.
Our ego's 'attention' is focused on 'judging, animosity and attraction,'
— 'pushing and pulling' everything in our life; so that we become weary
in our agendas and we are distracted from our real creative purpose, by
habitual, judgmental likes and dislikes in the ego, (that simply drain us).

Thus, we can be asleep to our soul's voice due to this distracting and noisy
agenda in our mind, and we grow only unconsciously and slowly,
and, all too often, we manifest anxiety in our experience.

Unconscious creation is what causes us pain. It is what we are leaving behind us.
But when our attention is placed inwardly on our soul, and on our Breath,
then our three Aspects can unify, even while we are on the Earth plane;
and we grow, and we can finally Create in Love, consciously.
Our *innermost* divine Individuality called our *Christ Self,* is a Word of God.
This term *Word of God* is used in scripture to refer to our individual
GodSelf. In essence, the Divine says, "I Am This I Am" or this One,
when expressing each of us.

We are a perfect Idea of individuality within Divine Being,
and we fit perfectly into The One and its Universal Expression.
Each of us has always been a part of Divine Being's conception of Itself.
This is why we are each an Eternal Being, and why our *essence is universal*
—because of this same Oneness.

This perfect Idea that we are is what we are living up to
even when we don't know it; and it is our Christ Identity,
a divine light image, to which we are each inevitably moving.

So each of us will eventually merge our awareness into this light form
of pure Individuality. We will each eventually arrive at 'becoming'
our true essence, as the 'Word of God' Self.
It is this Christ Self of our Divine Portion that unifies the work
of our soul, spirit, and body.

It is the Image of the Divine One inside of us that always leads us forward,
and will *become* our conscious Individuality in due time.
Our Christ Self inside God's mind is made of light.
It's a projected light IMAGE in Divine Mind.
We are actually permanent Beings of Living Light; and our Living Light
is what contains the energies of our soul, spirit, and body.
When working with these creative energies, we are working with Light.
Even here on earth, it is the material of Light through which we work,
though it may not appear so, due to its earthly density.
That which appears as earthly substance is simply a shadow of the material
of light, which is "stepped down" to visibility for our benefit.

Let us now discuss a more earthly perspective.
How shall we operate in *conscious creativity* and how shall we bring about
a transformation in our personal life? Let us look at our true day-to-day
powers and our real *personal tools* within.
How shall we really understand our Triune beingness?

Think of your soul, breath, and body as the ***Love, Faith, and Power***
of your daily Self (as you express all your activities moment to moment).
These three—your *love, faith, and power* create all your experiences in daily
life. It's where you point them in this instant that makes the difference.

You see, the love within you defines the "I" of your personal Selfhood,
and this Love naturally produces initiative toward that someone or
something that inspires your fondness.
Your love comes out as ***desire and inclination*** and you naturally focus
on the object of affection.

Now, your faith is embodied and extended as this *Focused Attention* and it also produces wisdom regarding your recipient of affection. Focused Attention radiates love, and this causes *Expansion.*

Personal Power is the resultant expression of initiating Attention toward whatever interests you.
Wherever you point your loving Initiative, and wherever you apply your faithful Attention, this is where you will find your life force Manifestation.

What do you constantly stare at or continually attend to in your mental experience? Is it joy, sorrow, a poor self-image, complaints, success, or nothing specific at all? It is this to which you give "body" in your life. You cannot help but give body to it; it is unavoidable. Remember this: When our three aspects of *intention, attention, and expression* operate within us in concert, anything can be achieved. And when we remove any one of these energies, the activity is soon to dissolve.

So our *Intentions* start in our love and inclinations. Then our continuing *Attention* creates understanding, and we *Express our ideas visibly,* no matter what they are or where we are. Your Initiating Attention is your true power, even though your Attention is invisible.

Without LOVE (without a sense of "I") there can be no Initiative expressed *toward anything;* and so nothing would be initiated.
Without FAITH (without a sense of, "I AM focusing on this") there is no Attention expressed, and nothing can be developed *without Attention Shining.*
Without POWER (without "I" expressed) nothing can be made manifest. We call our Divine Creative Process *Soul/ Spirit/ Body,* or "I Am I." I am This and I am That, I am.
It is where we place our energetic identification that manifests our creativity. This is the Infinite Life creating expression, as you. This is the Law of your wholeness and bliss.
SO...Unify Intention to Attention and you give out Expression. This creative process operates through you and as you. This is your true being and eternal creative purpose. Understanding and utilizing it, is also the conscious way to manifest a transformation out of our past choices— (*the Past* initiating our old 'attentions').

We, therefore, shall learn this: Our three energy aspects of soul/spirit/body manifest our creative power, when operating in Unison.
When in our daily life we work in harmony with our divine purpose—
in our Christed Awareness—our intention, creativity and expression,
work powerfully as one. Then transformation is possible and our efforts
feel timeless ... and bliss is felt in so doing.

However, if you are still unconscious of your Divine Beingness
and its conscious wholeness,
and while you are still "on the journey back" to integrating
your soul, spirit, and body .. know this one thing:

No matter where you are on your spiritual path,
no matter what your occupation or endeavor, no matter the state
of your Intention, Attention or Expression, I, your Divine Christ Light
am always with you. Yet you are free; and even if you don't believe it,
what you manifest is your business.

I AM ready to assist you in re-uniting your "divided" awareness
into purposeful power. For I AM one with you in Consciousness
and I can guide you into conscious creation
as I AM one-with The Infinite Living One – the Universal "I AM I"
from which we all emanate.

Think, have you not heard my Voice in the silent space of your heart?
Wherever there is three-in-one As one.. in your heavenly beingness,
This.. is your eternal Essence.. and it is the domain of your divine I AM I.
It is .. and ever will be in wholeness.

The Divine I AM is ever the One Expression supporting you,
and it is eternally calling out to those.. who feel separate.
(Please Answer by going within).
It only awaits our Conscious *'purposeful re-union'* and our willing return.

However ... wherever there are people "un-united in their beingness" —
with their aspects still apparently separate — I AM by their side.

And wherever there are people journeying aimlessly in life,
I AM always with them, no matter their beliefs ...
and I will be, even as they return Home   30.

II

LEAVING THE WORLD BEHIND

"I .. if "I" be lifted up from the EARTH [from the bodily ego nature]

then you will be drawn into ME [the Divine One, in your midst]."
John 12:32

I came into the world to understand your plight and help you.
So I appeared in a body of flesh;
but I found everyone drunk with forgetfulness regarding our Divine origin.
They were "hypnotized" by trying to satisfy sensual appetites.
They were not thirsty for the *inner truth,* nor knew what they were missing.
Then my soul was sorry for humanity,
because of the sensory programming of their subconscious minds.

They do not realize that as Divine Beingness sent into the world
they arrived here empty and unfettered,
and when they leave this world, they will leave it unfettered also.
Now they are drunk,
focused on poor self-images and sensory pleasure in the exterior world.
But when they renounce the wine of the senses and the external appetites,
focusing inward instead,
they will begin seeing the truth of Who and What they really are.
They will transform from this blinded state, in bliss, and will ascend
into conscious and loving creativity, even, while on the earth plane. 28.

One who has known the world and its ways has discovered it produces
an identification with the body as self, and a consciousness of self as effect,
instead of cause. It is an empty identification, which feels powerless,
and it leads one to the "corpse" state. However, the world-system cannot
restrain one who has discovered the Inner truth, *(that our earthly essence is
One-with Divine life).* One who discovers this truth will expand beyond
this world in the awareness that our conscious life and form are the
invisible and visible light – The I AM I the Creative Expressive Power—
which cannot end up in a corpse. 56

People think I have come into the world to bring peace to the world.
They do not know I bring division, to sift the true
from the false identifications in human awareness.
I bring a spiritual FIRE [the Divine Breath] to BURN away the beliefs
that there is "distance and separation" between Divine life and Human life.
I AM giving this spiritual FIRE *(awareness of breathing divinely pure Breath)*
so that ascendance over a body-mentality may be achieved and true
identification with Divine Spirit may be enjoyed. This true identification
frees our awareness, and reveals to us our Light Essence.

Also, I bring a SWORD (earnest, incisive intuitive discernment)
to SEVER the "binding cords" of limiting 'ego beliefs' from Living Souls.
Those who receive my SWORD are bestowed with the gift of Divine Insight.
I tell you within a person's *mental household* there's confrontation going on.
That is, within us there exists our three divine aspects
as a "Father Mother Child."
These three aspects are our *Soul purpose, creative Spirit, and self Expression;*
and these three work tirelessly, attempting to transform the ego's reactive
mental habits. Opposed to this transformation, there is also within us
the hypnotic, negative belief in separation to which man's ego, holds on.

Mankind thinks he lives and dies alone here in this world, that he is
cut off from everything *that everything is separate* from him, and somehow
opposed to him. He believes he is not one-with the Universe, but separate.
He believes he is incarcerated in the world, that he is inside the Universe,
not knowing he is an aspect of it.   It is a total belief in 'separationism'.

Mankind believes in duality. He believes in his mind and his ego,
and that he is in two-ness.
He thinks his body and soul are two distinct and different things.
He does not know that his within-ness gives birth to his without-ness.
He eventually will realize however, that he must unite his within and
without and that he must unify his Heaven and his Earth
if he wants to experience Heaven. He must bring a spiritual consciousness
to his fleshly work, to each thought and act, so that his outer life
may, indeed, be one-with his Inner Guidance.

He must work out his own salvation with reverence and submission
to his Inner Self. He must see everything as different aspects of this true
Oneness. He must realize that the entire Universe is alive with intelligence
and loving support, in a divine infinite variety, and with endless living
expression. He must see the Universe as his source and his ally..
and that *he is IT in expression.*

Until this is done, the 'unenlightened son' [*the two-ness of body mentation*] is
opposed to the Father's triune Oneness: [I AM I of Soul, Spirit, Expression]
So they appear to stand apart, this ego of flesh and this light of spirit, and
as long as "the son" has eyes closed to this truth, he feels weak and alone. 16.

One man said to Yeshua: "Tell my brothers to divide up my father's possessions with me." Yeshua answered: "Am I one who divides things up?" Looking at his disciples, he asked:
"Do I divide things up, or do I unify them?" 72.

I tell you, if someone believes his father and mother is of this world,
his belief shall make him an illegitimate child
of his Original Self in Heaven [of his Divine Consciousness].
For his belief separates him from his true origin,
and his opinion separates him from his spiritual sustenance.
If one believes that one is a human creature, he is tied to that belief. 105

Sadness comes to those whose identification is with their flesh
and whose individuality is tied to their ego-personality.
They hope that good fortune will somehow come to them like magic,
through some good luck, or that a Divine Being somewhere at a distance
will randomly or periodically "smile on them." They do not know
they must awaken to their interior powers and guidance, to unite
the leadings from their divinity within to their human activities without.
They must consciously unify their Father-soul to their human desires
and their Mother-Breath to their outer behavior. They must find the
blessing that soul and spirit bring to each moment of life's activity.
Without this unification, there is quiet sadness around the soul, because it
has no harmony with its unconscious bodily expression and is therefore
unfulfilled with unconscious creation. *Consuming the wine of the senses is an
attempt at escaping this sadness.* The soul hopes its fleshly persona with its
base identifications will at least moderately *sustain itself til unification occurs.*

I tell you, un-united with its true being, this earthly persona
shall remain under the power of its painful beliefs and its fate.
It shall be subject to time and chance, and it shall pay its uttermost karma
regarding these beliefs. But those who unite their "earthly doings" to that
pure consciousness in their Center. shall rise above their past debts.
For in throwing off the darkness and selfishness of ego-programming,
they shall ascend to a new level of existence in authentic spontaneity,
feeling bliss in each breath, and finding grace in each deed.
Then with that Inner Guidance of the moment, they will actually
leave their karma behind, and they shall take dominion over current
circumstances, with Conscious Creation. 112.

One who has known the world understands the limiting identification
the world has with the body as Identity. But one who understands
the limits and error of identifying self as the body, and as effect
will rise into the Divine Initiative of their Soul, becoming powerful
in Awareness, and will transcend 'the gravity' of the ego system. 80.

Here is a parable to illustrate how we should honor our Inner Self:
A SAMARITAN [*who to Israelites, was a second-class alien, minority person*]
was Carrying a LAMB atop his shoulders [was acting spiritual]
while WALKING the ROAD toward JUDEA
[while moving toward spiritual integration].

Yeshua asked his disciples: "What are the Samaritan's intentions?"
They said: "He will slay the LAMB later, then he will eat it."
Yeshua replied: "While the LAMB is alive, he will not eat it;
he can only consume it once it is dead." They said: "That's true."
[*While true spirituality is externally incarnate as Yeshua, people will not
seek out their own purified consciousness but will continually seek out his;
and this is why Christ Consciousness must be individually realized.*]

Yeshua said, "You too should be seeking rest on the SHOULDERS
of your I Am [in your Soul, and spiritual center]
so that you may avoid becoming corpses in this world
and becoming ripe for being eaten and then spit out by the system."

The meaning of this parable is this: *Each of us is the "Samaritan"*
and *the lamb* represents the purity of our inner spiritual Identity.
But we carry, or wear our spirituality for 'appearance's sake',
not really internalizing it, or living from it.
And as the SAMARITAN [*as the un-illumined person of this world*],
we WALK the Road toward JUDEA [*move toward our enlightened state
– 'Judea' – walking the path toward that inner "I AM joy"*].

We, like the Samaritan, are in fact hoping to receive acceptance
and entrance into the HOLY LAND [into our *blissful consciousness*].
So as we walk, we should take into our awareness "The LAMB"
to become one-with that gentle purity beyond ego-mentation,
by rising above it and thereby cleansing our mind of old beliefs

and old motivations. *"He who dies to this world shall live in Me."*
Drop the outer one; put on the inner one.   How do we do this?

We speak less. We still our self, becoming quiet. Stillness purifies.
We ardently listen, outwardly and inwardly, and observe the silent flow
of our feelings. We practice innocent activities.
We esteem teachableness and humility, like a meek lamb.
We do this by becoming un-entangled from worldly pursuits
and by taking charge of private moments.

So we must partake of our *light within* with eyes closed to the outer world,
feeling the expressive power of our soul's purpose, and of our spirit's work.
We must then drink the "pure blood,"
[nourishing our self with interior experiences]
by sitting quietly in solitude with our Deep Self, and feeling its reality.
We must focus within on "clear emptiness" in meditative reverie,
and we must now speak the "I AM" consciously.
Then we shall *consciously and purposefully breathe the deep spiritual Breath,*
for extended moments, becoming one-with the Infinite One
whose pulse permeates creation, and whose "exhale" expands the universe.
This purposeful and conscious breathing creates a fusion of our within and
without, and promotes a oneness of our breath, to our soul and our flesh.

This Breath allows our light center, the divine Self Awareness in us,
to clean us of old patterns, and to express itself.
It cleanses our cells, our heart, our body, and our brain of all impurities
by releasing its loving interior FIRE. Living life in this powerful discipline
becomes like swimming with a powerful current behind us.
Then our Christed soul becomes the GUIDE and the power of our external
persona, creating abundance, power, and peace in our lives.

Remember the parable: *Except a seed-shell rots away from the SEED*
when it's fallen into the SOIL, the seed shall not bring forth FRUIT
[bring forth its transformation].
It must let go of its identification with the hard exterior and its old nature
before it can expand and grow into its transformed state. Just so, if an
individual remains focused on the temporary body-personality of this
world, *and remains un-initiated to his divinely birthed true soul purpose;*
and if he remains unaware of the power of his divine Breath and its fiery
cleansing purpose, then in this life he shall simply age, shrink and wither

as the un-evolved ego personality he received at birth,
not realizing he was something magical.

So the system will eat him up in his striving in the ego-darkness
and he will die like a human.
However, when he attends to the Inner Life, he will live like a child of God.

The key is the *transcendence, expansion, and transformation* from the old ego
[*the outer personality's habits and identifications,
 inherited at our DNA birth and built up throughout life*].
Then his greater Self within will become his external self.

Our greater Self arrives by our consciously involving our
Divine Consciousness within us, to absorb the personality patterns of our
personal self, so that they may be used for their destined divine purpose.

You see, there is a seed impulse within each of us.
It is a motivating vision or divine template in our center of being
and it provides to us the desire of our heart,
'through which fulfillment' we experience bliss.

Look for this seed purpose in your life. Find this personal destiny
by searching your interior. Follow your blissful feelings,
and find the grace of your life path. Quiet your brain. Simply behold
the interactivity of life with your impulses, and it will lead You.

Each of us is made to shine in a unique manner, while serving the whole,
yet flourishing within our authentic purpose.
To realize the bliss of our divine purpose, we need to surrender
our identification with the small ego—those temporary personality patterns
we currently call our self, which contains empty appetites and protects itself
with defensive and constricting habits that only prolong the pain;
and forestall what is an inevitable realization of our divine Origin.

This surrender takes place in your conscious Awareness
[*when you've actually made a decision, in the quiet humble stillness
of your interior consciousness of Self*]
that you will **consciously partner** with Divine Being.

You will then be en.rapport with that intelligent, loving, expansive
life force in your center of being, and It will care for you
by empowering all that you do.
All of this occurs when you care for your mind and body,
producing purity in your activities. And by Breathing On Purpose.
Create purity on Purpose, in body, mind, and action. 60.

Then Yeshua summed it up saying:
Be passers by in this world...stay centered; focus on your inner self. 42.

III

THE GROWTH OF THE INNER CHILD

"Behold! I stand at the door and knock, if anyone hear my voice, and open the door, I will come unto him, and sup with him ... and he with me."
Revelations 3:20

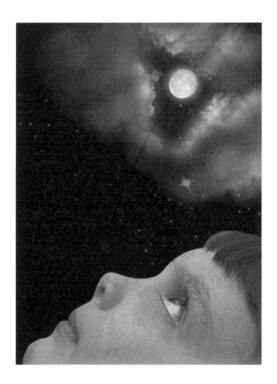

*O*ften you desire to hear the words I AM now expressing to you.
But days will come when you will have no one to teach you,
and searching for me shall not find me.
So through your powers of observation, you will discover your pure
awareness within, where your Spiritual Presence is, and you will become
one with it, and you will attain wholeness in the single One
[within your loving and infinite presence].
Then you will experience bliss and clarity of purpose in this world. 38.

You see, being human is like being a skillful FISHERMAN.
The fisherman casts the NET of his meditative focused attention, into the
SEA of his infinite Consciousness within himself *[into his Source of ideas]*
and he draws out of this SEA *[out of his mind]* many SMALL FISH *[his
attention is cast upon unimportant subconscious thoughts, beliefs or opinions]*.
However, if the wise fisherman discovers among these many "thoughts"
the LARGE FISH *[discovering I AM Awareness* in his own consciousness],
he realizes that The Divine lives in and as one's very own Self; so he throws
the smaller fish *[lesser religious ideas]* back into the Sea and focuses only
on the fact that his being is in fact Divine Being living each moment.
Then happily and peacefully he focuses on this greatest truth and it
becomes his moment-to-moment guide and his ever-present reality.

So with joy he continually contemplates this one expansive truth
as he lives each day.
If you understand about this constant contemplation, then do it.   8.

Disciples asked Yeshua: "When you, who are our spiritual teacher, leave us,
who shall become the leader of our group?"
Yeshua responded: 'When you have left behind your old idea of self
and have unified your soul and your flesh, your morals and your activities,
and like an athlete have melded your mind and your body —
and your purposes and actions — so that you make an integrated,
harmonious presentation of yourself in word and deed,
then shall you arrive at a State of Grace, becoming justified, becoming the
earthly BROTHER of your inner Soul...in the PLACE of
the OLD MAN identity [the former identifications with ego].
You will then be a CHILD of LIGHT, who needs no human leader to
guide you." This is the Reason why this whole system of heaven and earth
came into being. 12.

His disciples asked: "*After you're gone, when will you appear again to us, and when shall we see you again?*" He answered:
"You shall see the Christ again when you see it within your own Presence.
Yet a little while and the world shall see me [*the external Light*] no more [A]
but YOU will see me; For the I AM and the I [the Lighted Consciousness]
will make our dwelling place, in You and your individual Awareness." [B]
When you finally shed shame and guilt from your awareness,
it will happen. When you stop thinking about mental concepts of God,
pondering Divine Being itself [*becoming aware of your soul's voice*],
then you will experience this true Self.
Take all the old thoughts about spirituality, which you wore mentally,
which like old clothing draped over beauty, concealed from your awareness
that graceful Living Being that you truly are.

Now then, cast away the old conceptions of God from your mind
and trample them joyfully under your FEET [*under new understanding*]
This may take time and experience in solitude…
so apply yourself to its unfoldment.
Replace old identifications by *living differently*
with a new routine of activities in each day.
Then build on these new activities, always adding new patterns to your life.

True spirituality is not about simple church going but a loving interaction
with your Divine Being within … and your neighbor without,
who also is a manifestation of God.
Develop a new schedule for each day *rather than one not benefitting you now*
This will create beneficial patterns for you to grow with.
Building new patterns allows you to leave behind old, unprofitable ones,
until you can live in now.
You will then rise above the old inculturated patterns, as you rise into the
spontaneity of now. Then, like a child in summertime, you will be free.
You will then see the *Child of the Living One inside your own Self* Awareness
and you will see your Light Being [*your Divine "I"*] as your true Identity
and *you will no longer, serve that ego-persona* and its restricting enslaving
habits. Then fear will no longer be a part of your consciousness. 37.

His disciples said: "Your brothers and mother are outside." Yeshua answered:
"Those who live and act from the expansive Consciousness within
are my true family. They enter into the divine HOUSE [our inner being]
as I do and they reside where I reside." 99.

He who does not love more his heavenly I AM—his soul and spirit—
his Mind and Breath — over those who are called the earthly father and
mother cannot follow me into the expansive realm of our divine beingness
due to their worldly focus and those in it.
But he who does not love those here, who are called dad and mom, as I do,
cannot be like me and do as I do.
For they must love the Divine Life in everyone.

My earthly mother brought me into this world of death,
but my heavenly Mother [my Spirit Breath] gives me life eternal.
The two are one, but the heavenly is greater than the earthly. 101.

Simon Peter then spoke up:
"Mary Magdalene should leave our inner group, Master,
for the nature and requirements of this life are too difficult for a woman,
who is beholden to others and encumbered with many things."

Yeshua reproved him: "*Women are just as worthy as men.*
I shall lead her, as I have you, and add unto her the MASCULINE aspects
of the soul—loving purposefulness, single-mindedness, and initiative—
that she may enter into expansive Awareness,
becoming one-with that initiating soul-state as you all are just entering, too.
"For any woman who balances herself with the masculine nature of the
soul, *as any man who balances himself with the FEMININE side of spirit—*
— wisdom, nurturing, and creativity—and becoming unified,
shall enter into the expansive Awareness of their unified soul/spirit/form
and They shall find.. their divine destiny.

They shall consciously exercise divine initiative, creativity, and expression
in this world; and they shall operate from
Purposeful Love, Wisdom, and Power." 114.

Whoever cultivates words from my mouth inside themselves,
whether male or female, shall become as I AM;
for there is no partiality in Divine Being
and the I AM within him or her shall become the Higher Identity *in them.*
For them, the mysteries will reveal themselves,
and they will come to know the truth in all things. 108

But they pointed to a GOLD COIN in the basket of a nearby tax collector
and said to Yeshua: "*But Caesar's men endlessly tax us. How can we ?*"
He replied: "Render unto CAESAR [the world system] what belongs
to Caesar. Give it its requirement. Making war on the Roman system
causes pain and potential death.
Do not create new pain trying to change it for your own ends;
For your kingdom is not of this world system, anyway."

Change your awareness of self, be born anew in consciousness,
re-identify with your breath not the body; and your 'kingdom'
shall transform right before your eyes.

You cannot even comprehend the bliss created by the beauty that exists all
around us, right now. And so, you shall help your brothers more in this
manner, than with any ego struggle in the outer world. Those are for egos
to keep themselves busy .. engaged .. but you .. keep focused within.

Then, You shall become a Light to them, and you will help them rise into
their own bliss. Then they shall help others, too... and it goes on and on.
Each in their own time will find and live their truth.

Therefore, render unto God *[your Deep Self]* what belongs to God
[your inward focus] and give to your Christ Identity what belongs to it,
this TEMPLE persona to govern. 100.

IV

THE PATH OF GRACE: FRIENDSHIP WITH THE DIVINE

"Seek first the consciousness of God, and God's purpose for you, and all things shall be added unto you." Matthew 6:33

*F*rom morning to evening and evening to morning do not THINK fretfully about your external life.
Do not THINK anxious thoughts about food, money, appointments or any of the things concerning your outside world.
Fretfulness brings you down.

Yes, your inside is the key. Focus on your interior Presence while living each moment; for that is what is truly living and experiencing your life.

Talk to The One every moment. because it is a Universal Presence, and can perfectly respond to every situation you encounter and manage life gracefully. This *feeling of your Presence shall guide you* with blissful feelings in the moment.

Consider this: Who by THINKING fretful thoughts about any thing can make a balanced and appropriate choice regarding it?
Who can operate from a higher plane of Awareness when in worry?
Who can act in enlightenment when they have not yet entered therein?
And Who can move with confidence when standing in darkness?

The expression of Creative Power comes not from hoping but from knowing. It recedes away into un-confidence, in painful darkness, when fed by worry.
Power and confidence do not emerge from wishful thinking or uncertainty, but from the expression of our unified being which operates from the power of love. Therefore, listen now for the Secret of living life.

It is the power in love's attention that effects newness. Love is the Secret for transforming your present level of awareness, to illumination.
It begins in pointing your loving radiant attention toward your Inner Being, where you find Freedom in Conscious Choice Making, and it brings you purposeful power.

Attend to the feeling, knowing Living Presence in your Center with love [your radiant Attention] and as you live each moment focused there, all outside responsibilities that need taking care of shall in fact be handled naturally. You will not have to worry over the little things, and the necessities shall be taken care of with power.

"Your I AM Self—in whom you live and move and have your being" [C]
and "who dwells and walks and talks in you" [D]
"knows what things you have need of;
your I AM is not in the dark about your life."
It is divine pleasure to care for and feed you. [E]

You are a divine child, currently in an earthly expression
yet tenderly watched over.
You have too little faith in the Loving Power of your I AM
and so much faith in trouble and limitation.

What good can come from believing in trouble?
When attention is placed in fearful negative thinking,
it limits you and your life.

Expect the best. You're going to expect something anyway,
you might as well expect the best.

As a Child of Infinite Power and creativity, your attention is indeed
powerful. Your I AM has granted you, the "I" expressed—dominion
over your personal world, to manifest whatever you hold feelingly .. and
breathfully in consciousness.

It is ever radiating Divine Power, which flows through the LENS of your
Imagination and your Attention, to project your assumptions into being.
But it is you who directs your attention. Attention is the Secret Power
of love, but it is You that focuses your attention.
What is it that you hold in your mind? To what do you give your attention?
What images do you constantly hold of your life in your conscious
and subconscious centers?
What you see manifest as your personal life is the out-picturing of your
deeply held vision of yourself and your life, even if you don't believe it.

The having of a MIND and its focusing purposes are Your responsibility.
Take seriously your power.
Show prudence in choosing the beliefs you hold feelingly and the images
you hold continually of yourself in consciousness.

Remember, without an understanding of the Divine Law of love,
that love focuses your attention,
it is impossible to divinely pleasure the Divine One
who wishes you to consciously express his power effectively and lovingly.

For when we believe in love's radiant Attention,
love becomes visible as manifestation takes place.
Creation occurs as Love radiates Attention.

Just as confidence breeds more confidence, it is also true that when we
ascend into our Deep Self, our loving Creative Awareness,
Divine Love and Creative Power are expressed in this universe more often,
but they come through us, which creates Divine Pleasure, as the Divine
has another avenue of expression through which to work powerfully.

So you see, *your Divine I AM is always doing all it can do for you*, and
always will. God will not be doing something for you tomorrow that God
is not already doing for you today. *Divine Attention always shines on you.*
It is your attunement to the Divine Awareness deep within your
consciousness that creates your answered prayers, your success and joy.
It is by Altering your "held" self-image *to alignment* with your Divine Self,
that creates bliss.

When you ponder grace, grace occurs. The Divine experiences your bliss
and has continuous pleasure in your growth. God loves your
expanding Awareness .. especially your oneness with Him-Her.
It is Divine Power that rushes in to fill up the mold of your innermost
expanded assumptions and to *manifest your new understanding.*
If you spend time imagining and feeling your oneness with Divine Being,
then it is that Image that God shall manifest in the outer world.
It is your choice to focus on what you will.
It is your decision to hold onto the feelings that direct the flow
of your spirit, which in turn manifests for you according to your faith,
— that vision that you hold of yourself and your life.

Yet, there is a higher way to live and there is a path of grace. There is a
deeper friendship with the Divine. It comes by trusting your Infinite I AM
who loves you more than you love yourself, and letting It guide your day.
If you find that trying to govern your universe and life is exhausting,
then let go. Listen on the inside to your divine intuition, and obey it.

How? *Just do what seems the appropriate thing to do in each moment.*
And do whatever feels peaceful. Remember:
With inner quietness and confidence, you will always find strength. [W]

If you focus continuously on your **all-loving, all-providing
spiritual Vibration within, you will stay in touch with bliss.**
If you permeate your awareness with the graceful power of 'I Am One'
you will see Divine Grace manifest throughout your life by its guidance
of you. Any unpleasant conditions *manifested so far in your life* will drop
from you, since their existence lived only from your attention anyway.

Your staring at painful circumstances only keeps them with you.
Do not stare at your current negative situation. *Go within yourself daily*
to feel your oneness with Divine Being and obey God's leading from there.

Let your *heart-centered feelings* regarding each moment of the day
and each activity, be your GUIDE as to the appropriateness of your
thoughts and deeds.

If your heart remains peaceful before and during an activity,
instead of anxious, then you do well.
Trust that your life is actually being guided, and it will be.
Practice friendship with the Divine by listening to divine leadings.

'*Acknowledge God in all your ways so God will direct your Paths in bliss.*' [F]

'*He shall keep him in perfect peace whose mind, thoughts and imagination
are stayed on Him*' [V]

Look within all day long as you look without,
and your Divine heart leading will direct your steps.

Follow your feelings moment-to-moment and let blissfulness be the guide.
By doing this, your heart shall rest in peaceful oneness, and your mind
shall be filled with lighted Awareness.
But it is .. a continual dedication. 36.

When you allow the Divine Individuality inside you to express,
what you allowed will expand you.
If you do not allow this within you to express, once again
you will TASTE the STING [the unconsciousness] of death. 70.

V

THE PATH OF ASCENSION:
Uniting Spirituality with the Outer Life

"If anyone thirst, let them come into Me and drink; For one who believes in Me out of his belly shall flow rivers of living water."
John 7:37

[From his center will flow self-sustaining awareness that feels his life force and creative power in motion; and feels a love that fulfills itself by blessing all]

*D*isciples then asked: "Do you think we should practice fasting,
and how do you want us to pray, and… how should we distribute offerings,
…and are their rules to be observed in eating?" 6.

He replied: "If you fast out of habit, or as a ritualistic duty,
or in self-righteousness, you have missed the point of fasting,
which is to willingly and cheerfully release any thing or any activity that
prevents your attention from being focused on your divine guidance
within. Focus on the essence of I AM—fasting from thought—
then your mind will grow quiet, then, you can truly hear.

"If you attempt a food fast and fail to honor either the letter or the spirit
of it, you will then judge yourself and will have created a SIN for yourself
[literally a *"missing of the mark"*].
"Fasting from food provides dominion over your bodily appetites and
passions, which is a necessary step and a profitable one to take.
It cleanses your bodily systems, which is also necessary.
But it is not an end in and of itself, and it does not create righteousness.
"However, fasting from old patterns and unconscious self-centered habits
is true progress."
Regarding prayer, if you pray out loud to be seen of men, in a public show,
you may be judged by others as self-righteous
and public words would not be honored by your inner being, anyway.
Public words only "serve your ego," which exacts its own price,
feeling false rewards. [G]
Many words do not make a prayer. But just this—I AM—
can move mountains of trouble.

Prayer is not made with the lips
but with the utterings of the heart in its yearning for oneness.
True prayer is accomplished in inner privacy,
in the secret place of your soul and spirit. [H]
When you are in communion with your soul [your elevated consciousness]
and when you are one-with your spirit [the universal cosmic Breath],
you then rise above the ego state as you enter a Divine Silence to create.

In your divine center, you rest from your personality
and you are in touch with peace. In prayer, you calm down.
Release your worries. They prevent entrance into your soul state.

Rest peacefully in prayer, in confident expectancy, knowing it is a
divine pleasure to give you the whole Consciousness.
True prayer creates a delightful integration between
your personality awareness and your breath.

In truth, the answer to prayer exists before the prayer is made,
and it is yours before you claim it.
Your desire is its herald, your vision its promise.
Effective prayer concludes with *confidence* [with resolution that is felt].
In powerful prayer, we "see" or "feel" the outcome of the prayer
inside our being, and this creates a joyfulness.
Then we feel that it is "already accomplished."
We realize the Divine Presence *has gone ahead us, to accomplish the purpose.*

It is when we feel that click of joyfulness.   But do not undo it all later on
with anxiety, worrying over it. Your joy is the sign, and your peacefulness,
marks its certainty. When Divine Being feels inner peace and gratitude in
you its power is released. This is because your inner unification occurs.
You see, your Soul [*Divine Will*] unites with your Breath[*Cosmic Creativity*].
Then ever-Radiating power and ever-flowing divine substance move into
your inner vision [the joyfully nurtured interior event]
and its manifestation is brought out.

Create by becoming one-with your desire. It is a realization and a feeling.
Prayer is not about asking for something or saying "I want."
The result of prayer can only be *your wanting.*
Wanting is a state of lack—but gratitude is an experience of being whole.
You shall have whatever you really believe. Prayer sees and feels it NOW…
not then. Don't put it off. Everything is actually one with you already.
See it, feel it, claim it, smile.   It is all here now in the invisible.
We make it visible by attracting it to us within.

You must create consciously if you wish to escape your past.
Prayer is about the present, not the future, Not Maybe but creativity Now.
It is divine joy to co-create with a conscious you;
unconscious creation can be painful.
You are a door from Heaven into this world of matter, into this
world of experiencing. You are the outlet for creation.
Desires arrive by coming 'through you'.

Know this, prayer is unlimited and effortless.
It can be offered up all the time. It is for quietly expressing gratitude in
every moment of the day. It is in every moment that your
divine **Father-Mother** [your soul and spirit] provide your life and breath,
your consciousness and creativity and all things in gracefulness.
So say "Thank you" at every turn, *everywhere* in any moment.

Now, when you give OFFERINGS from religious duty or outside pressure,
it is not from a heart of benevolence, understanding, or cheer.
So instead of receiving a blessing from giving, which is divine law,
a baptism of emotional pain is felt at being forced.
But when true giving occurs, the gift is given cheerfully
to your Deep Self—to God, *in the other person.*

And God is constantly replacing the gift and giving a hundredfold
to her children in return for their sharing with each other.
So give where it is needed, where the gift will be felt, giving with personal
attention, for your Divine "I" loves the thoughtfulness of this strategy.

And wherever you go, whenever you travel, and hospitality is offered,
eat what is set before you and aspire to love. Do not argue over food.
It is not what goes into your mouth that defiles you,
but what comes out of your mouth in painful creativity.
Help others in whatever way you can. Stretch forth your hands
and heal any sickness among them with your warmth.
Speak your words in loving kindness, for their pain may be great. 14.

Grapes are not gathered from thorn bushes, and figs are not picked
from thistles. Just so, a good man brings forth excellence from his heart.
But an un-united man, living backwards, in shadows and selfishness
brings forth condemnation and pain from his ego nature,
speaking negativity when he communicates himself. 45.

Therefore, do not practice lying about yourself or others.
Speaking the truth energizes your spiritual growth
and reinforces your ability to focus the light of awareness,
which discerns between human perception and truth.

Your soul always knows the truth. It is everywhere. Rely on that.
Lying is injurious, most especially to the one who lies.
Speaking truthfully allows you to make positive accomplishments in rising
above the worldly ego nature, which is all the time rehearsing deception.

When you stand in truth, you "face the sun" and you allow light
[true Awareness] to clean you of shadow areas in the ego persona;
**those mental and behavioral habit patterns that are constantly seeking
reinforcement and repeated validation, that consistently
make slaves of the children of earth**, who are under their dark and
heavy burden.   Arise and throw off the bonds of deception and "sleep,"
which maintain that stagnating, primitive ego facade.

Take the first conscious step. It is all important. **Wake up with Intentions.**
Because *the first step of your ascension* toward Self [*toward your interior life*]
is the death knell for the old life [*that external focus on ego appetites*].

Don't do things to others or yourself, OF Which you disapprove,
because it breaks down your centeredness, and causes contradictions
within yourself .. that have to be cleaned out later.
Don't agitate your consciousness *Practicing deceit*, but let it soar with
integrity. Your participating in deceitfulness only pulls it into Your life
(for you to deal with). Doing things of which you disapprove only adds to
your burden, and causes you to use universal and personal energy painfully.
Follow the admonition:
Don't do what you want …then you can do what you like. [I]

The fact ever remains, in a universe founded on truth, light, and
Omnipresent Consciousness, everything done in secret, for good or ill,
will be shouted from the HOUSE TOPS
[**will be revealed by and In your Face, Words and Person**a].
Everything hidden will be revealed, and nothing covered
will remain undiscovered. For as it is within, so shall it be without. 6.

It is a blessing when a destructive ego-appetite is consumed by one's soul,
because its transformation into spirituality provides a new sense
of dominion that is unsurpassed on the path of personal growth.
Even the pleasure of one's cherished talents do not compare to the pleasure
of feeling this dominion. But it is abject sorrow when the awareness of soul

is consumed by one's uncontrolled appetites, because then, non-awareness
and inner pain, will sadly, be continuously experienced .. and feelings
of worthlessness and hopelessness can run rampant within one's being. 7.

So look to the *Living Consciousness within*, that formed your body-temple,
beats your heart, breathes your breath, and receive help, rising into dominion.
Do this as long as you live, lest you die in this world "under the thumb"
of ego patterns, then start searching for him inside Eternity,
at the outset feeling failure. 59.

Then they said: "Well come master, and let us pray today and fast".
Yeshua said: "You say that as if there were a particular sin to be removed.
I AM always fasting from the world system,
and I AM in constant communion and prayer with my 'I AM I' within,
— listening to its leadings.   It is absolute bliss to do so".
You see, if one has lost touch with one's spiritual I AM — that heavenly
bridegroom to one's earthly persona — then indeed let one FAST from
ego patterns, for extended periods of time if necessary, in the wilderness
of solitude, and let one PRAY powerfully, to recollect one's True self. 104.

Some disciples asked him:
"Is circumcision a truly needful or *righteous* thing to do?"
He replied: "If it were useful toward your transformation out of ego,
the Divine Mind that formed you would have circumcised you from birth.
However, the circumcision of ego-impulses and down-pulling habits
has always been beneficial and always will be.
The *preserving and focusing of sexual energy is the real meaning of
circumcision*; take up that discipline "of preserving-focusing sexual energy,"
if you desire powerful growth".
That energy is awesome for transformation, used properly. 53.

I say unto you *pitiful is the body-personality sustained solely by food and drink
without the nourishment of the soul,* and its now-moment guidance.
Sad is the soul whose body remains non-integrated with its wholeness,
whose aspects remain *half ..in sensory pleasure seeking*, and not Whole. 87.

Then he said: "Honor the Divine Life within you,
which was unified before you became two weakened halves.
Because if you follow my example and hear my words,
truth will spontaneously rise up within you, serving your Awareness,
to make you Whole again.

This spontaneous and beneficial interior Assistance will bless and surprise
you to no end. You will feel like a favorite child,
and you will smile incessantly."
There are 5 TREES — WAYS [5 yogas (unifications) or life systems]
on the spiritual path for one to practice everyday. They are: *Loving service*
— *Faithfulness* in word and deed — *Knowledge* gathering —
Discipline for breathing, mental cleanliness and *action for conscious
evolution* and finally, *Worshipping* [going joyfully within to silently listen
and commune with your divine Soul-Mind].

Practicing these five activities raises your desires above self-centeredness
and leads you away from sleep-inducing ego habits.
They place your focus onto truly living and onto your inner beingness,
as opposed to habitual patterns and the beliefs of the outer world.
And in neither the 'summer or winter' of your life
will these activities lose their fruit of transformational effectiveness.

For the person who practices all of them, a special nourishment shall be
bestowed. They will feel self-sustaining Divine Life moving
within them each moment, and they shall not TASTE death
[*make life-transition unconsciously*]. And they will avoid assigning to
themselves another life of confusion [in non-awareness] in which
struggling to Awaken to our true Identity, occurs all over again. 19.

Why do people wash the outside of their life, washing their external body
and affairs, and forget about cleansing their inside with Silence?
For the purity of mind and heart is the true purity,
and it is cleansed in the silence of solitude.

Do they not realize that the outside of their life is soiled
because of the uncleanness and distracting noise of their mental world?
Do they not know their mind is soiled by participating
in worldly activities? 89.

We see the small character flaw within our brother's persona,
but we do not see the massive personal flaw within our own.
Once we have overcome our weaknesses and begun to see our true Self,
we can help our brother see his. 26.

Remember, *when the blind lead the blind, they fall together* in the ditch. 34.

One's spiritual persona is not honored in public.
A Prophet is Not honored among his friends.
Just as physicians do not generally have good friends who are
willing patients, one's spiritual Identity is not taken seriously. 31.

Do not give the sacred to dogs and do not speak your truth to those
who care not for it or who will mock you,
for it's casting what is precious to the dung heap.
Just as you would not *cast pearls before swine*, for they would destroy them,
do not place your spiritual energy or precious truth out into the public eye
of skepticism and ridicule, to those who are uninterested and undeserving,
for you could be the one injured. 93.

Love your neighbor as your own soul
[for your soul is one with all neighbors]
and cherish him as your most beloved treasure. 25.

VI

~◈~

LIVING AMID
THE CHALLENGES AND TESTS

"There is one body and one breath,
one Lord and one faith, one baptism, one God and Father of all,
who is above all, through all, and in you all."   Eph. 4:4-6

"I and the Father are one."
John 10:30

*B*lessed are the POOR
[*blessed are people Not driven to manifest the values of this world-system
in their life's heart-space — like those always wanting more;
operating from an empty sense.. of lustful ego-power and pride*].

These will not be burdened with the self-made troubles
of unconscious creation in their life.
They shall have a rich and peaceful heart, being fulfilled in their
awareness of Soul, which delivers its loving influence continually,
all the way out to their physical life and daily awareness. 54.

Blessed are the ones who have come to understand suffering,
for it appears to be a mystery.
They learn not to rely on the outer world or its comforts,
for their peace and consolation.
They truly discover the warmth and reliability of meditating upon
their Inner Being and upon the truth:
'Consciousness is expressing my Awareness from deep inside myself' 58.

Count it a blessing if people persecute or hate you, and truly, if you're
beaten, for they assist you, teaching you not to look for your good in
the outside life. Actually, they eliminate only the pride of the human
personality when they torment you. But the purity of your Eternal Self
within, remains and shines through. 68.

Blessed are those who have suffered from being persecuted in their heart
[where their I AM Presence is] Who feels with them and comforts them,
in their solitude; And who,
because of this shared experience, is felt by them.
Blessed are the hungry for that soul guidance within;
for if they seek after it, they shall be filled and satisfied
and will ascend above the mundane weaknesses of the ego. 69.

When your teachers talk about the arrival of *the Kingdom*
[*the consciousness of bliss and power*] and if they say it is an external event —
and that it will descend from the sky, you will know this is untrue, because,
if it was an external event, then the birds in the sky would arrive in heaven
before you, the Divine Child, would arrive.

If your teachers falsely claim this Kingdom is off in the future, you will
know this is untrue because then, your descendants would arrive *before you.*
These common teachings are error, because Now is the acceptable time,
Now is the day of salvation, not then [K]
The truth is Now is the only time we have, and Here is all there is.

The Kingdom of God is in Power. It produces a sound mind,
and it is for your edification now. Remember, it was said,
"*The Kingdom of Heaven* [the Expansive Awareness] *is at hand.*" [L]
It is because it is here, Now, right where you are.
It is inside your own being, for it is your life.

The Kingdom of God [Divine Domicile] is within you. [M]
It is in your very PRESENCE. [C]
It is the living, breathing, feeling, Creative Consciousness being you —
guiding you, shining out from you, and living you. [D]

You are one breath with God. There is no outside to Divine Being.
This Divine Essence is also without you, omnipresently existing
everywhere, in everything. [R]
You are in the Divine Presence wherever you are;
whether you are in the desert, the sea, "the Hell of human thinking"
or at the gates of the GRAVE;
even there, your Christ Self shall hold you [the earthly persona].   [N]
But it is no farther away than your own consciousness and breath,
for you are The One. When you know your Self, YOU will be known.
You will know that you are an expression of your invisible I AM —
that you are a PORTAL between Heaven and Earth. [S]
You will know, as I do, that I AM is the DOOR, I AM is the truth,
I AM is the life, and I AM is the WAY to the great I AM I. [O]

This mystery of *God's divine oneness with us,* is the secret.
For what could God express from, but His/Her one Infinite beingness.
There is not God, and something else. There is only God.
So you see, this is why I speak not of myself.

The words I speak are not my own.
The Divine Presence within me, He speaks and He performs the works,
and my I AM sends me and I obey. [P]
So if you do not know your Self, you are in poverty and you are poverty.
If however you do know, you shall be a power-point for The All,
and you shall source healing. 3.

Show me THE STONE [the spiritual Truth]
which the religious leaders rejected,
and I will show you, the CORNER STONE [Primary Truth]
of our Divine teaching and you will see that it is a spiritual Identity
within humanity... that is our very life.
You will then know that our Identity of Light is our permanent Self!

Our Identity, is a Divine Light Child. It is the I AM individualized as "I"
but this "I" is one with an Infinite "I AM" which inhabits everything,
including our being.
This Infinite One is beyond your human mind, in back of mentation.
It precedes your thoughts, judgments, emotions, and rationalization.

This Living One is discovered in your Breath and in Consciousness itself;
for It actually envelopes, permeates, and interpenetrates our human form,
our life, and our ego-brain, living in the past, with which we contend so
often [and on which we needlessly place so much of our daily attention].

In fact, this Divine One inhabits our entire universe –
here, there, every where .. and in past, present, and future.
God's Mind holds the essential reality every where ... in everything:
in you, as you, and always in every way, and in every where.

This is your destination.
You must find this essence of Self to know your bliss.
To find that Center of consciousness within your Self, pause, rest,
and start feeling.

Find that Movement and Rest ... every moment as you breathe.
It is your Original State and it is your initial, primary stage of being. 66.

VII

REUNIFICATION: YOUR DISCIPLINE AND DESTINATION

"You shall know the truth, and the truth shall make you free." ~John 8:32

*H*is disciples asked him: "Tell us how our end will be?"
Yeshua said: "Do you really understand your origin, that you can now
ask about your end?
Our end is the same as our beginning. They're both found in God's Light.
You came from Light — Living Awareness,
and you are Light — Conscious Divine Awareness,
and to this Light you shall return."

Blessed are the ones who know their beginning,
for this is their permanent Home, and they shall not TASTE death.
Not TASTING death means not making transition in a "sleeping" state
and experiencing it as many do, unconsciously, without conscious consent.
Many are unaware and are unwillingly Carried obliviously by the 'current'
of their old awareness and their old belief system..
to a dimension where similarly unaware and like-minded souls congregate.

In this way, by practicing principles that foster Divine Awareness,
one will not fall under the power of one's former non-awareness during
life transition, but will go to the LIGHT fully conscious of the process,
and the destination. 18.

An OLD MAN [*the ego persona in one*] heavily burdened with beliefs
about separateness from God, will not hesitate to ask a NEW CHILD
of Divine Awareness – only seven days old and freshly REBORN, about
the wondrous Presence emanating *in him*...and how he happened on it.
Then that "Old Man" shall find the same Place within his own being,
he too will transform, and There he too shall Live.

Many who appear in "first place" in this world shall transcend last;
and many who have appeared to "win the prize" here...
have actually lived in pain and sorrow [*residing daily in their ego mind*]
and have experienced separation from true Love, in their Soul
and perhaps shall be the last to see the Divine One in their Center.
For why should they seek their Center when it has always been confused
with painful human thinking and discontent?

But one day, they too will discern the difference between
the Love of and In soul... and the hell of ego-mentation [inner pain].
So eventually, all individuals, will see the Truth of our being,
and ALL will be united within their Infinite Divine Presence. 4.

Then he put forth a question: Consider this:
If the bodily flesh came here to serve the breath, that would be a mystery;
but if the breath came here to serve the body, that would be a miracle.
Do you know why such wealth makes its home in such "apparent" poverty?
If you do, then you know that Individuality and Embodiment are the
Divine Intent; and that the maturity gained through embodiment,
regarding mercy, with its evolved and mature wisdom,
are the benefits of incorporating consciousness within a body.
Also, the deep appreciation that our earthly experience provides to us
regarding bliss, when it is juxtaposed to the Painful Grace,
which comes from human suffering,
makes one realize that Individual Embodiment, is The Divine Way
of sharing with us, the Greatest, richest, most salient insights on being. 29.

No individual Living the Truth, *high* in the MOUNTAINS of Pure
Consciousness [*within his true Identity*] can fall; nor can he conceal himself.
For when one *attains unification* with the Living Spirit [*the conscious Breath*]
and realizes the Wholeness and Power of operating from one's
Unified Being, one is not able to hide that fact.
However, remain MEEK [teachable] and HUMBLE [wisely allowing]
so that Awareness *will arrive.* 32.

Then he said: Whatever you understand in Full Awareness, *knowing it
within and manifesting it without as well,* you may teach "with your Mouth"
to the truth-seeking children; and as The Mouthpiece of I AM,
you will bring them new Awareness.

For as no one lights a lamp in order to place it UNDER a Basket,
neither will The Divine enlighten an individual to keep them shut up
or keep them away from the world.
They are put on a "stand" [in position] to let their INNER LIGHT shine
so that all who ENTER or DEPART this world, may see and know that
LIGHT and *Also* have the opportunity to experience true Awareness. 33.

If you understand that your origin comes from Infinite Divine Light,
where everything originates, then what is hidden will be known by you,
and you shall know that you Are, and that you ever *Will be.* 5.

When you look into mirrors, or see your image in a picture,
you are interested in your image.
But when your *Mind's Eye beholds your personally held* MENTAL IMAGES
constantly rising before you, neither subsiding nor approaching,
what will you do with them?

These private thoughts endlessly hover around our consciousness.
They haunt the mind, arising from one's personal hell of "thought taking,"
anxiety, or worry. They are bolstered by FEARS and NIGHTMARES,
and by a fretful, negative Imagination.

How long can you withstand the pressure of this inner pain?
When will it all be enough?
Why will you not surrender the Mind's focus back to the I AM —
the blissful place — instead of in anxious mentation?
Continual inner communion is what I speak of.
I AM Awareness is where your life is *peacefully maintained* and truly utilized.
Take no anxious thought for "not now – not here thinking".
Sufficient unto today are the adversities thereof.
Therefore, let him who is willing listen now and act appropriately!
Remain in the present moment – in pure I AM awareness, always just here
and right now. Let go of all yesterdays and their sorrows, they are gone.
Let go of your tomorrows, which are not yet in awareness.
Living today in wonder—in the now-moment—creates blissful tomorrows.
Count your blessings. Enjoy and be thankful for all that belongs to this
moment, whatever it is, and be enthusiastically involved in that activity.

Let go of control. Stop trying to run or 'pattern' this life after mental
fixations and egotistical agendas.
Stop the endless criticism of yourself and others, even in your mind.
Let everyone be… especially yourself.

Let peace flow between you and others, and between your thoughts.
The I AM will provide whatever you need to learn from experience.
You are the judge of no one, so let judging go away from you.
And be gentle on yourself.
However, give yourself some disciplines to refine your nature.
As you do, your refinements will become you;
they will *give birth to new growth,* ever new expansion, and new disciplines.

Your greatest endeavor is in Loving yourself—and others—through
loving expansiveness. You actually Assist others on their life paths,
and your own as well, by taking charge of pointless appetites,
which make others stumble as your lives touch.

Your Expansive Kindness, however, inspires other people's lives
with a love from Above.
When your love goes out to others, it returns again to you a hundred fold,
becoming the Grace to you that it was to them.

In doing these things you become a clear LENS and a clean VESSEL
through which the Original Being may work the wonders
of the Infinite One ... in you. 84.

There are many at the threshold of their I AM awareness, but not realizing
how to enter; yet only the 'Solitary Ones' enter into this bliss, entering
without an agenda of "me too." Only those who have *united* their
soul, breath, and body into a singleness of purpose—whose
Intention, Attention, Action are united in surrendering the *"me too ego"*
(toward rejoining the Oneness)—
will reunite with the Living One, within themselves consciously.

These shall enter the BRIDAL CHAMBER
[the divine temple/Consciousness].
These shall join together the NEW HEAVEN [the new spiritual Awareness]
with the NEW EARTH [the newly developed Body] within their life,
and shall become the embodiment of divine peace,
[becoming the "Jerusalem" consciousness in their Individuality].

This means your LIGHT Consciousness *is wed to the earthly temple;* that is,
the BRIDE GROOM [your Christ Mind] takes residence with the BRIDE
[*your divine Breath-Breathin*g] which gives birth to the Child of Light
and its life within your earthly form, as you are then "born from Above,"
and you become the "Son of Man" who understands this truth.
So do not become a person known for their much 'talking'
who is always at the door of Heaven, yelling "Let me in,"
when there is room for only *The One.*

When will you be done believing in your separation from Divine Being,
as if there is you and It?
Hear plainly, Children of the Divine:
Divine Consciousness is your consciousness.
Divine Breath is your breath.
The Divine Heart beats your heart.
The entire life of our divinity is One life—in a Oneness,
and it is expressed in infinite variety.

There is no one else, besides God, anywhere. 75.

VIII

THE KINGDOM OF HEAVEN:
Our Ever-Expanding Expansive Awareness

"Be you transformed by the renewing of your mind."
Romans 12:2

*D*isciples challenged: "So tell us what the Kingdom of Heaven is like."
Yeshua responded by teaching them the symbols of the Kingdom:
The expansive Divine Awareness grows within your heart
just as the incredibly small MUSTARD SEED grows in a GARDEN.
Although it is the smallest of garden seeds, it eventually becomes
the largest, most expansive life in the GARDEN [of your heart],
so that all the BIRDS of the AIR [your intuitional spiritual thoughts]
will make their home in your now-moment Awareness, giving you bliss.

It may appear that spirituality can be crowded out of your awareness
by other PLANTS and WEEDS
[worldly thoughts, dogma, misinformation],
but it grows beyond them, and surpasses in size, stature, and life force.

Then all the activity of your heart is overshadowed and blessed
by the expansive Life Force of your purest inner Awareness,
which will transform the nature of everything within and around you,
providing an inexplicable constant cheer. 20.

Any path, system, philosophy, or endeavor conjured by the human ego
does not have inherent life in it; so if it is not tethered in the Truth that we
are one-with Divine Being, it will be torn at its roots and inevitably die. 40.

However, when a Spiritual Messenger comes into the world,
he spends his life planting spiritual SEEDS [words/ideas] that have a
deep spiritual root and feeds all our hearts with the spiritual life
of our oneness with God, which is eternal.

The SOWER casts his words across the **Ground** of many listeners' hearts.
A few words fall upon the ROADWAY where busy people and bystanders
listen a moment but, disinterested, continue their daily affairs, and forget
the words quickly. Other words fall upon hearts who, though they listen,
are filled with a love of money and lusts of the world, placing their
attention on pursuits that do not nurture the new words that have fallen.
Still other words fall upon GOOD SOIL [open receptive hearts] where the
words are like LEAVENING *[catalyzing* 'spiritual seeds'] and they expand
the listeners' awareness of their I AM Life Force, allowing divine experience
and knowing, true peace, and unconditional love to flourish. 9.

Awaiting the full bloom of this individualized Expansive Divine Awareness
is analogous to a full SEASON through which a FARMER [God] waits,
because God has sown GOOD SEED of truth in the FIELD of your heart.
Yet among the Words of Life, the 'world' sows WEEDS in our Heart-SOIL
  [negative identifications in our consciousness; such as painful
  self-images, desires for money and worldly things, laziness, jealousy,
  greed, gluttony, violence].
Such addictive patterns and habitual weaknesses make humanity maintain
its attention on the body, the personality, the world, and on satisfying
temporary appetites, *instead of on the Life of the Inner Self, the truth & inner*
divine power. It is as if the world is trying to make us forget seeking our
pure Awareness and to stop attending to our soul, wherein,
we find our Permanence.

But the FARMER [Infinite Being] knowing the strength of His seed,
that it would not be choked out by the WEEDS, but would grow beyond
the weeds, said, do not worry over these WEEDS
[the erroneous beliefs in their mind].   We will not upset the progress
of new spiritual growth already present in their awareness.

On HARVEST DAY
[on the day they transcend their ego identity, in the FIRE of the Breath]
they will enter into EXPANSIVE AWARENESS instead,
and our good SEEDS will Expand, and the WEEDS [old belief systems]
will be uprooted and burned in the FIRE of realization.
So, when the FIRE in consciousness comes, the root causes of the ego life
[those misidentifications and mistaken beliefs about Identity]
will be cleansed out of this experience.
Therefore, look for and be prepared for your Spiritual Fire
[*in your spiritual Breathing*].
It will arrive for every person at his own divinely appointed time.
It will be a day like any other, except that moment will be like dawn.

Just as sun rays awaken the earth in the morning from its cool darkness,
so will that moment be In You — which reunites Light and shadow,
Spirit and flesh, and the " I AM " to the " I " – within your individuality;
On that day your inhale and your exhale shall be as one, and the power

of the Fire Breath shall transform your earthly body to a Light Body —
a body not restrained by earth and its gravity.
On a day when there is marrying and playing, and working and eating,
IT shall come; in the hour when *personal disconnected thought-taking* ceases.

And at a time, when you see within your heart, a vision of your True Being,
the transformation will occur in you, and the Child of Light
will take its place in you.
Then you cease from being '*MAN whose breath is in his nostrils*'.
You will cease this fruitless scheming and fearful mentations.
You will finally rest within your Divine I AM
as your Christed Awareness permanently replaces this limited mentality.
This removes "the veil" from True Insight and you *see into The All,*
And it will unravel the mysteries and purposes of all things. 57.

Maintaining your conscious spiritual Awareness requires the care and
vigilance that a SHEPHERD [*one who has a conscious evolutionary path*]
has for his one-hundred SHEEP [for his life's spiritual priorities].
The person who has a spiritual path tries to live consciously, and on
purpose, so he exercises disciplines over mind and body in order to create a
good life. However, among most people [*shepherds*] those with a conscious
spiritual path the most important dedication [*sheep*] has been left behind
and is missing. It is the true Idea of real living, that of witnessing the Christ
Mind operate one's life. This is most often missing from human awareness,
even from successful human awareness, even from rich people who enjoy
earthly abundance; because normally, the ego wants to run our life,
fulfilling its own agendas, despite our spiritual longings.

So the WISE SHEPHERD [disciple] does not focus on the 99 things of his
life so that he may find his Christ Identity ... and he will do that, until he
finds it. After all his searching efforts, when he finds his Authentic Self, he
will say, "I love you, my Christ Awareness, more than the 99 other things
of my life [*more than religions, possessions, philosophies, careers, wealth, fame*].

With everything in proper priority — with our Christ Consciousness in
ascendance, *we can attend to all of life's matters* and better than before. 107.

The Expansive Awareness within your heart SERVES you like a WOMAN
[*like your Holy Spirit's nurturing guidance*]
who adds LEAVEN *[transformative awareness]*
to her BREAD DOUGH [to her child of earth]
so as to BAKE a hearty large LOAF [a powerful child of God]
creating a loving, wise, and powerful Child of Light.

If you understand about this inner Breath assistance,
then receive this *interior help* and grow. 96

Faithfully focusing daily Attention on your spiritual Self cleanses your
interior being and empowers you for your journey Home.
It has to do with maintaining a true focus.
It is likened to a WOMAN [*our Holy Breath's nurturing Wisdom*]
who is carrying a JAR full of FLOUR MEAL on a long JOURNEY,
[*like our inner Spirituality carrying an ego full of worldly concerns
while walking through the human life experience*].

When the JAR HANDLE 'breaks,' something happens.
The FLOUR MEAL streams out BEHIND and is left on the ROADSIDE
[*when the ego's controlling grip is broken through our letting go of old
identifications, old fears, and old judgments regarding our self and our life*].
Then we are freed of the weight of these energy-draining concerns.

Now, because our Attention is turned AWAY from the past and its
negativity, our spirit's creative capacity does not continue producing
unpleasant manifestations. By and by, it is not noticed that the Jar's
WEIGHT *[the ego's burden]* becomes LIGHTER
[*our tendency not to notice our own progress*].

However, upon arriving HOME
[*to the Christ Realization that "my Father and I are one"*]
that Consciousness is one-with Expression.
Then we set down the JAR
[we *completely surrender the ego identification*] and find, it is empty. 97.

Acquiring the expansive spiritual Awareness is analogous to a merchant
who discovers that a truly rare and priceless PEARL
[*our pure interior Energy*] is available for his creative use.
So important is this pearl to him that he SELLS all his POSSESSIONS
[*ceases the practice of scheming and thought-taking in the ego*]
then he goes and BUYS the PEARL
    [lives by feeling and developing the Spiritual Energy of his Heart Center,
    rather than relying upon the continuous thought life in his mind,
    and that true heart focus becomes his life's power].
Seek like him, that TREASURE within your awareness of heart,
which does not fade, nor crack, nor depreciate like material wealth.
Find true riches in the permanent I AM Consciousness within your
Deep Self, where no moths or worms can enter to consume or corrupt. 76.

Achieving the Expansive Divine Awareness requires personal fortitude and
persistence; because a person must eradicate the ego's imbedded mental
patterns and personality habits that hide our pure Awareness from view.
But this eradication of ego patterns is accomplished by looking to our
inner Fire to burn these patterns out of our daily life.

Your Fortitude and Persistence is focused inward. This inner focus will do
the eradicating of our ego patterns. The small will-power of the ego mind,
when it's directed toward ending its own habits, ***is not where we find the
power to transcend.*** That power is found in our Divine Soul.
So this person practices utilizing incisive discernment into his own nature,
to discover its *currents and shadows, to find his weaknesses and temptations.*
He brings all his powers of focus into the Home of *his divine Breath
awareness,* to know as much about himself as he does about his profession.
This way *he can live each moment freely without being run by his ego's agenda.*

He practices employing a decisive WILL to focus his Attention on
Divine Being within, And in doing so will delete his ego's ingrained habits
one by one, as they are observed in consciousness.

He does this to develop excellence in his life—striking DEATH BLOWS
to his old habits and old identifications; such as pessimism, fear, and
laziness; which only serve as road blocks to transformation.
Then one day, his ego identification is simply eliminated altogether. 98.

The HIDDEN yet ever-present nature of our inner I AM
is similar to a man who is ignorant of a TREASURE [of Divine Being]
hidden in his FIELD [*hidden in his transpersonal heart-level awareness*].
When he dies, his son INHERITS this same Lack of spiritual awareness,
so that he too is unaware of the TREASURE within and, not knowing better,
SELLS the FIELD [pursues money and worldly things].

However, the BUYER comes [*the one on a Spiritual Path arrives*]
and while working continuously on daily transformations,
discovers the TREASURE [*the Lighted Beingness within himself*
giving explosive power to his spiritual endeavor]
and he esteems IT above everything worldly, and allows it to express,
and IT will benefit many,
and he himself receives More from its daily Increase. 109.

Having prepared a banquet, Divine Being sent his SERVANT
[*the soul's voice of guidance into the awareness of humanity*]
and he summoned the invited GUESTS — the most Aware leaders
of humanity's culture. So the servant went to them and reminded them
of their invitations to the divine BANQUET
[*to the inner heavenly Consciousness*].

Well-placed people often respond to their Spiritual Conscience like this:
"I have to advise some merchants in my debt, who are visiting me;
I cannot come." Others say: "*I have bought a house and I must care for it.*
I have no time." Others reply: "*I'm sorry but my friend is getting married,*
and I must organize a celebration dinner.
I'm too busy for spiritual disciplines."
Still others respond to their Intuitive Spiritual Guidance with the excuse:
"*I just bought a business and I must collect accounts payable today*
that are very important."

The Divine Servant [our soul's voice] comes back to our Divine Life Force
unrequited, reporting that the guests are not coming and are too busy
with worldly responsibilities to spend time with their God.

So Divine Being responds to its Soul Desire, saying:
"Then go into the streets and byways and make yourself known
to the common folk and invite them.. to partake of their Divine
Consciousness [they HAVE the time]; *for they will lead well-placed people*
into the Consciousness of bliss and power. The weak shall lead the powerful,
the poor will guide the rich, the dumb will confound the mighty,
and a Christ Child in their Center shall lead them all into the dominion
of a divinely powerful life, in joyful liberty."

People who pursue money, things, and worldly power do not enter the
Consciousness of their Divine Interior; for they are too busy to come in
and sup with their Divine Mind. They are too pleased with their earthly
affairs to know Me, or to find true joy, liberating light, or the true power
of Divine Love in their lives. 64.

A rich man with a great fortune decided to expand his wealth even more
by investing and selling and investing again; that he might fill his bank
account to overflowing with money and assets. He did it to feel secure and
accomplished, and to gain even more recognition. However, that very night
he died in "monetary darkness" – *poverty stricken in spirit.*

Let him who under stands, fulfill his Divine Purpose of knowing God
while he IN the world. 63.

One who is rich in this world attains many material things
and can become a "king"; but one who is powerful within needs nothing
this world offers, and joyfully transcends it — in spiritual awareness. 81.

If you have monetary wealth, do not lend it out at interest
but give it to them who will not need to repay it.   95.

Let it be a gift, given cheerfully and without mindfulness of virtue. (X)

He who has found the world and its riches should remove himself
from worldly activities and pursuits, to find his Original Divine Identity
and his real purpose in the world.
If you have money, use the opportunity it provides,
to find and know your true Self.

How much simpler can it be? Use the opportunity that money provides
to find your Divine Beingness; and when you do,
you then have the monetary power to do real good. 110.

Disciples asked: "So, Master, when will the rest for the dead begin?
And when will the New World appear?"
He answered: "The Divine Interior Sanctuary that you're expecting
is already here, although you do not recognize it.

The Divine Kingdom is spread out all around you right now.
You are already in it. You live in Divine Mind.
You are never alone, and you are enveloped in love.

Love is at the center of all things.
The Divine Kingdom of YOUR God is WITHIN you.
Rest in that knowledge as you live and breathe." 51.

IX

LIVING DAILY
THE LIFE OF TRANSFORMATION

"I baptize you with water, but he that comes after me is mightier than I and he shall baptize you with the Holy Breath and Fire." [lightened Inner purification]." -John the Baptist, Matthew 3:11

*Y*eshua said: "I shall destroy this HOUSE
[this present Consciousness-Temple].
I will leave it behind and nobody will be able to restore it.
Although I – *the Christ* – to teach you about the power of pure Awareness –
will raise it up again,

I can pick it up or lay it down, for I express this earthly image
and I have power over what is called life and death."   71.

His disciples asked him: "Tell us about the place where you live,
for we will seek for it if you teach us how."
Yeshua said: "Let him who understands this Mystery, act on it every day:

There is the light of the Divine One within us.
 It is a Divine Awareness in our center, which guides our daily living.
It is where we experience wisdom, joy, peace, love, and power.
These qualities shine from one who daily immerses himself meditatively
in this inner Living Awareness, and he naturally shares this loving light,
impartially, with everyone in his world.
"If he does not share his interior light, there is darkness
out here in his world.
For darkness is an external focus in '*living* the world-system';
But Awareness is attending to .. and communing with his inner light.

Our purpose then is to BRING LIGHT [bring healing Awareness]
to DARKNESS [to human confusion and pain]."   24.

Now, the day you discover your true light [*your Divine Awareness within*]
your current idea of spirituality will PASS AWAY behind you,
feeling like another life or a dream. Your present belief systems and
old identifications will also pass away behind you.
Your unenlightened ego-persona will no longer dominate, as you've
removed attention from it ... and your rediscovered one true Self
will no longer pass through the sleepy transition of "death".

You now remember, that once when you practiced good habits —
when you practiced spiritual disciplines to enter your I AM Self —
it was you, [the one who believed in separation]
that put forth effort and allowed an unfolding expression of good works.

But when you reenter your Divine Light, and your expansive Awareness,
who do you suppose will be the ACTOR then, who will be the DOER,
and WHO will be doing the allowing?
Will it be the ego self, feeling separate, and alone — burdened with
the emptiness of the past...? Or will it be your Divine Beingness
acting from the Loving Power of the Present Moment?

In the beginning, when you were one-with "I AM I," you became "two"
by falling "asleep" and you dreamed of a "separation" from your
Divine Identity, believing the God Life Force to be someplace else,
other than in you, *as* your body and soul.

You dreamed that EARTH was separate from HEAVEN, and you focused
on the outer world's shadows and circumstances and dreamed of death
rather than knowing the power, present within your being.

But now that you are "two" [in a divided consciousness of half-ness],
how shall you return to The One, The Only, The Whole?
How can you rejoin what you never separated from,
or come back again to what you never left?

To awaken from your dream of exile, you must reorient your Awareness
of Self, by seeing your flesh as the *outside* of your breath,
and, unifying your divine impulses with your human actions.
Let your mind be the servant of your SOUL [your pure Intentions]
and let loving kindness replace ego's self-centeredness
[by continuously gazing within].
Listen to and touch the Divine Consciousness in your center of being
moment to moment, and obey the guidance that you receive there.
Listen.
You marvel at the things I do and the words I say, but marvel not.
The works I do and the words I say are from the "I AM I."
The words I hear the I AM say within, these I say;
and the works I see this Divine One do within, these are what I do.
You see, it is only a matter of attention and obedience.   11.

Then Yeshua said: From ADAM
[*our first 'governing' stage in the divisive "I am this body" belief*]
to JOHN The BAPTIST [our *final stage* in this divided belief]
at no time has there been any phase in human experience,
nor any incarnation in this unawakened human condition,
which was more evolved than the Awareness *embodied in John the Baptist;*
for even his name means "from death into Divine Grace."

This Awareness, [personified as John] signifies our impending rebirth
into true Awareness. As this state, *precedes* the Awareness that the
Divine Life Force Is our human life force. So this *old awareness,*
[this belief in perfecting our humanity with '*human Will'*]
eventually fades away. Even so, this '*perfecting' stage,*
symbolized as John the Baptist, remains unexpressive of the truth
that the Divine Presence, is our human presence.

So after this stage exhaustedly transpires, soon enough,
we Rise to the higher level of Identity.
Anyone who enters the solitude of his Divine Being within,
and waiting there, becomes SMALL and HUMBLE in his own eye,
but he will glory in submission.

Then, listening, he OBEYS the "still small voice" of God
within his consciousness, [and FOLLOWS the guidance given]
and then ASCENDS into his own Divine Awareness,
and finally ATTAINS to his True Self...
[*Above the temporary "John the Baptist" beliefs*].
This means, he rises above his need to 'perfect his personality,' with the
new Idea instead – that of spiritual surrendering– *surrendering to a superior
Truth,* and a Superior Self Awareness...NOT to a superior power.

The Old stage of 'will power' must be SACRIFICED.. before this arrival
of Illumination, and it disappears from our concerns, with the arrival
of the Awareness of Light ... AS *our Consciousness and Body.*

We relax into a new Identification, into our Divine Original Awareness,
which takes over *operating* our **Temple Identity Life** in the spontaneity
and authenticity of the now-moment. Then, our Identity,
simply manifests its perfection, instead of us "trying for it." 46.

Then Yeshua saw little babies being fed and said to his disciples:
These babies being NURSED are like those being nurtured into
Divine Consciousness by their Holy Breath.
For these babies work to receive their food, yet their mothers work as well.
They replied: We are humble.
Does that mean we can enter into Divine Consciousness?

Yeshua said: When you, with childlike innocence and complete acceptance,
see The One in everything and everyone, as well as yourself;
and when you make the two *[your soul and body]* as equals,
also when your inner life is honored equally with your outer life;
and when you make what is without like what is within,
 — making your external activities like your spiritual guidance;
and when what is within is just like what is without,
 (as when your thoughts and words match your actions…)
and your Integrity is clear;

When you unite the male and female ASPECTS of your being,
uniting your Power and Wisdom, so that your male Soul aspect
is no longer unconscious, unbridled force and your female Spirit aspect
is no longer unconscious, compliant creativity,
but each, henceforth works TOGETHER, at cause and *consciously.*.
by attending to, and *following* your Divine Guidance within;

This too…When you eliminate DUALISTIC "seeing" from your mind,
[*thinking that good and evil exist separately in the Universe of Divine Being*]
When you eliminate your beliefs in SEPARATION,
(***ending your beliefs in a judging, condemning Go****d*)
who lives somewhere outside of you, in a distant locale called Heaven,

And replace those beliefs by seeing with the SINGLE EYE [the One "I"]
that sees One Loving Power in you, and the Universe,
in emanation and concealment – not Two powers in opposition;
and when you believe a Divine activity permeates all your affairs,
instead of believing that Your life is only *your* Life,
(in limiting your life experience with willful schemes and self-centeredness);

When you cease this endless constant defending of yourself and your ways,
but rest, instead, in a quiet state of being;
and when you enjoy true understanding, and therefore peace,
because you have given up judging life, *solely from appearances;*

and when you have let go the ego's habit of criticizing all about you
but live peaceably instead;
When you see **oneness, wholeness, and Divine Love** between you and every
thing, instead of seeing incompleteness, weakness, and separateness:
and if you nurture This Gaze and This Attitude within your Heart,
while allowing the Healing Breath to *nurture and expand your daily Vision,*
then you shall enter the Expansive Being of your Eternal Self. 22.

If your soul and flesh make peace within your conscious life and living,
and if you unify the spirit/emotion with all your *thoughts, words, and deeds,*
your unified Presence can command any life challenges to "give way" and
they WILL MOVE; for the power created by the unification of *intention,*
emotion, and *love's radiant attention,* is greater than any earthly situation
that you could encounter at any time. 48.

A man cannot ride two horses at the same time, or accurately shoot
two arrows. A servant cannot obey two different masters;
he must honor one or the other, or they will put him at cross purposes.
No one drinks in the OLD WINE of *old religious ceremonies and rituals,*
then immediately desires the NEW WINE of *inner spiritual inspiration.*
For until one leaves behind the old beliefs of separateness from God,
one does not appreciate the freedom and grace of attending
to the inner Self Awareness.

Nor can the Christ Awareness be contained in an OLD SKIN
[of the 'ego personality'] because it would break apart.
For the old identity, impure in itself, cannot withstand the power of *Divine*
Beingness overshadowing it. One must increase one's vibrational frequency
with breath work, exercise, meditation, and proper diet.

This raising up of one's Light Vibration allows the Christ Mind to perform
its work within the body. Conversely, old awareness is not found
in a purified body-temple for the temple could perish from the poison of it,
due to the debilitating nature of that old awareness.

Just as an old patch would tear if sown onto a new garment,
the old ineffective lifestyle of the former ego identity
is not suitable for the New Man Divine Persona. 47.

When you make the two into One, **uniting your breath and your flesh -**
daily in new powerful ways - and when you WED your soul to your mind-
- **intention to thinking**—you become the spiritual Offspring of humanity.
You will be called a "Son of Man" because you will be a member of a new
Divine Race on Earth — the next stage in human evolution — and
you will be a citizen of a new generation. Like a prince born from among
peasants, *your Consciousness will be powerful.*

Then if you order the MOUNTAIN to move [*if you command your*
elevated and powerful Consciousness to serve you], it will. 106.

Your Christed Awareness and your old self-image share each day and each
night within you. They share the FOOD eaten and all aspects of your
living, until the final moment.
They even share the bed on which you sleep—
but One shall Live [the *Divine Awareness* shall live]
while the other will die [the **ego persona** will be risen above].
On that day of Transformational Rebirth there shall be two in a bed;
One shall be taken and the other [the ego] will be left behind.

There shall be two in the FIELD [*Two "identifications" in the heart*].
One shall be taken, and the other [*the ego-memories*] will be left behind.

Then Salome, thinking the Christ Awareness was only true for Yeshua,
misunderstood saying "Did you at some time sleep in my bed, Master?
Or have you eaten from my table?" Yeshua answered her:

"I, the Christ Light that you see, *the Divine Life in Yeshua,* am actually,
the expressed Life of God, that is in all people; *'I'* am an equal in Heaven'
[*Individuality is an integral part of the Infinite Consciousness*],
and it is one-with the Infinite I AM of the Universe —
— it is an equal and individual Aspect of the Infinite One —
and is given all things that belong to the great and infinite I AM."

'I' am in equal honor, because 'I' *is the Visible expression of the I AM —*
and each of us is this expression.
This 'I' [*this Christed Awareness in each of u*s]
is the One Child of the Living One in every person.

Each 'I' is the One in the Many, and the many in the One.
'I AM' is the Infinite, expressed in diversity."

Salome then responded: "I know why I am Master, I am your disciple."
Yeshua replied: "But listen. When a person is growing equal to their divinity
[raising the person's light vibration], they are filled with their own *Divine Awareness* and is suffused with tolerance, wisdom, and love for everyone.
Also calm understanding, gracefulness, freedom, and power
will *flow from them.*

So they do not need a master, except of course the Infinite I AM,
who is awakening us to that Oneness in each of our individual lives,
and who is our very Life, heartbeat and consciousness,
and our One True Cause.
"But when a person is going away from his *Divine Interior and Natural Self,*
[toward his self-centered ego-personality]
pursuing momentary pleasures, things, and self-centeredness,
his awareness is filled with worry, frustration, and confusion.

He feels self-doubt, vacillation, and darkness,
because he regularly avoids the Love within his soul;
and this is why he regularly condemns himself and others.
All of this creates pain, violence, and sorrow.   61.

X

THE TEMPTATION: WHOSE TEMPLE IS IT?

Yeshua In-Breathed with them and said:
"Receive you the Holy Breath." ~John 20:22

*T*hen he said: I AM casting a FIRE upon the world [*the Divine Breath*]
to purify, nourish, and transform the race.
When humanity discovers this Fire Breath, they will transform their earthly
body to Light. I rekindle this awareness until it BURNS us into Light
beings everywhere [until Divine Breath purifies everyone]
and all of us, as a single Divine Child, ascend into the *One I AM.* 10.

He who is close to Me is close to the Fire of Divine Inspiration,
for it transforms the propensities of the physical form and the ego-brain.
He who is far from Me is distant from that healing, transforming Breath
and that enlightening Spiritual Awareness. 82.

ADAM, (the human phase in the evolving Divine Self Awareness)
arrived here with great power and abundance; taking authority
over the earth scene, utilizing great ingenuity in subduing it.
Even so, he, as an evolutionary step, is not adequate to express
your capability, your power, or your Divine Heritage.

As a stepping stone, the ADAM identification
is not deserving of your continued attention; as Is the Christ Mind,
who is your new interior master and your next stage.

The distinction of a master is his loving life force and his power.
Had the ADAM PHASE been truly advanced with breath and body
united as a Conscious Force, he would not have "*tasted death*".
But the divided human awareness identifies with the body as 'identity',
seeing itself as separate from Divine Life and separate from the Breath.
Ego believes the Spirit Breath is something that passes in and out
of the body, instead of seeing it somehow being 'One and the Same'
as our Human Life.

Your Divine Awareness, however, is of Wholeness —
— of Heaven and Earth, within and without, spirit and flesh as One.
It is a Oneness ... and it transforms livingness into lovingness. 85.

Then Yeshua — the Christ-**Man** – the embodiment of pure individual being, asked his disciples, "Compare me to someone. Tell me whom I resemble?" Peter replied: "You're like a righteous angel."
Matthew continued: "Or like a wise philosopher."
But Thomas said: "Truthfully, Master, I cannot bring myself to utter comparisons to you."

Yeshua came to Thomas and quietly said:
"I am no longer your master.
You have drunk from the bubbling Fountain of Life which I brought,
and now you are drunk with the discovery of your Spiritual Breath
and of Divine Being within your heart,
which from now on will lead you and from now on you will obey."

Then Yeshua took Thomas aside and gave him three words.
[Probably a mantra, such as "I AM I" – the Divine Name,
to reinforce and strengthen Thomas's newly formed consciousness of self].

The other disciples came to Thomas asking: "What did Yeshua say to you?"
Thomas replied:
"*If I told you the words he gave to me,*
you'd probably be shocked or you would become belligerent or
argumentative, and would hurl STONES [spiritual truths and principles]
At me ... accusing me of blasphemy, whereupon FIRE
[the purifying divine spirit-breath teaching that Yeshua gave them]
would rise truly from the STONES [from your arguments about Truth]
and your arguments about Truth, would inevitably point to this Truth
Yeshua gives, and your words would BURN and Indict you instead." 13.

Then some of those disciples said to Yeshua:
"Tell us who you really are, so that we may believe in you."
He replied: "You are testing the FACE of Heaven and Earth.
You are studying *The All* [the manifest universe]
without recognizing the Divine One that inhabits everything and everyone.
You do not see God, literally everywhere. But you do not even know how to truly live in just this moment, *without* an agenda.
"When you finally see *'The I'* within yourself, you will emotionally melt in joy and you will know that the *I AM and the 'I'*—Its manifest expression—are One. If you have seen *'the I' within,* you have seen your I AM Self. 91.

When you perceive one not born of woman
[seeing the Christ Expression perform its work within you]
then lay Down your ego personality and its mental habit patterns,
with which you have identified and protected all these years,
and just let them go. STOP leaning on your old habits.
Live spontaneously now, in the moment, without an agenda, and you
will be led by the Divine One, and you will live in the frequency of Bliss.

Humbly honor only that birth-less and death-less Divine Life Force in you.
Worship That One ... with time spent together .. within.
Make the purification and vibrational increase of your Temple [body]
the first priority; for that is the first glimmering of re-union
with the great I AM of you, in you, as you. 15.

"I the **Divine One,** am the Light. "I" am the true Self Awareness
and Expressed Image everywhere; and it is "I" that shines throughout
the manifest universe, especially in humanity. I AM I.
The ALL came from Me .. the One Self and incorporeal Life.
I AM divine cause, creativity, and expression in *unified* operation.
I AM living everywhere in everything. Now The ALL [*the external expression*]
is returning to ME, becoming Aware of Me.
SPLIT WOOD [*look between each of your thoughts and your teachings*]
and I AM there, within.
RAISE a STONE [esteem truth] and you will find Me everywhere." 77.

Come to Me ... for my yoke is Light [my admonition is Self awareness].
My leading is gentle ... and in Me you shall find rest and comfort. 90.

Then they said: "*Master, you must Be the* ... You are the one all 24 prophets
of Israel spoke of ... They have prophesied of *you* all these centuries."
Yeshua replied: "**You are still neglecting The One, who lives in your Presence
in order to talk about the dead.**" 52.

The disciples said to him: "Why do you say that to us?"
Yeshua replied: "You do not understand the I AM from what I say.
You've become like the Jewish philosophers who love only the words,
the study and discussions – [the philosophic system — *the TREE*] –

but they hate the growth and the transformational nature
of spiritual living [the fruit]."
"You love the FRUIT of the Kingdom [*the benefits of Divine Awareness*]
but hate the path of within-ness, and its discipline of focusing on God
to dismantle ego patterns, [*those habits and identifications you have ingrained in your consciousness*] and which you still think of, as your identity." 43.

Here is a parable to illustrate: A virtuous LANDLORD [Divine Being]
owned a VINEYARD [*the visible universe and the human Heart/Temple*]
which he leased to TENANT FARMERS [*to the children of this earth-life*]
so they could TILL it and develop FRUITS from the LAND
[*develop an Awareness of spiritual oneness in their Heart and Mind*].
Then the Landlord would receive FRUIT from them as PAYMENT
[*receive an evolved and spiritual awareness from his Individual Expressions, – His-Her children*].

Then Divine Being sent a SERVANT [holy man, guru, or prophet]
to remind them to make PAYMENT [to develop spiritually];
but he was seized, beaten, and almost killed.

When the servant returned to tell his master of this,
the Landlord thought, perhaps they had not recognized the servant
so he sent another, but they beat up him, too.
Then the Landlord sent his Son, thinking they would respect his SON
[*that growing Divine Awareness within their hearts*].
However, their egos knew that '*indulging an ILLUMINATION*'
[*from the Begotten SON-ship*] would be the end of the human ego.
So they KILLED him [*ignoring their own inner divine awareness, pointed out by the Begotten One*].   So, friends LET GO of your ***addictive ego-habit-persona***, while you are in this world, and RISE into letting your Christ Self express, while you are still within "Time." 65.

Blessed are you if you know the TIME of the ROBBER'S ARRIVAL—
— knowing when and where TEMPTATION comes in your life —
and, where, in your life, the BATTLE for dominion most likely will occur.
Which... shall rule over your consciousness, the world's attractions
or the Divine Life within you?

When temptation comes, turn within and ask your spiritual Beingness
to lift you out of it and *change your desires.*
Breathe deeply to calm your nature. Turn away from the temptation.
Do not continue to *look upon* the unclean thing *even pondering its qualities.*
Do not lean upon your own will power to overcome it;
at best, it's temporary, and this is because it is still
of the ego's mental structure,
and it does not draw you closer to your Divine Soul Awareness
but reinforces your beliefs of a *separate* strength and supposed *aloneness.*

Doing these things, you can prepare yourself and rise in meditation,
and collect yourself in prayer, and unite yourself in the deep, rhythmic
Conscious Breath, unifying soul and body as One Power.
Then you can stand prepared against the ego's temptations. 103.

Remember, nothing can enter your Temple Consciousness or upset your
life's progress if you are unifying your inner spiritual awareness with
your external activities. Nor can your life be seized by any force.
The Father of Lights has given dominion to each of us over our own being.
There is no need to worry over dark forces or spirits threatening your life;
it is, in fact, they who will shy away from your Light.
Do not fear anything invisible.
However, if your *inner spiritual activities* [your RIGHT HAND]
and *your outer earthly activitie*s [your LEFT HAND] are at cross purposes
and in conflict, then your current progress [your mental HOUSE]
can be ransacked.
Remember, if our Heart is divided against itself
it cannot stand unified, in strength.

Live your true and highest Awareness, and you will be a fortress of Strength
Do not live in contradictions, but abide yourself in pure
singleness of Purpose. Do not try living "spiritually" for only one day,
and live the other days otherwise.

Do not go against your "conscience" [*a pure messenger of God*].
Raise your vibratory level every day. Go within yourself to Feel
your Higher Self's wisdom-choices ... and Rest in those. 35.

He that has the understanding of *Oneness With* shall continually receive
or *experience* that which he is One With.. through the Law of Attraction,
whether it be spiritual or physical.
But to him that has not this truth of Oneness-With, even the things
he currently possesses he shall LOSE, through the
Law of Disassociation, and the Principle of Repulsion. 41.

If we repudiate or deny the existence **of our I AM Self** *(our Soul and Father-*
cause — **disassociating our human persona from our divine Beingness**)
this Can be rectified.. and we can experience an interior forgiveness
in heart and mind; because.. our Original Cause and True Being
are unaffected by our human ig*Norance.*

Now, if we hate or ignore 'the body' of our *current spiritual state* [the SON]
and if we belittle our current expression [*bemoaning our life situation*]
or complain over our *current unfoldment* and abilities,
We Can correct this too; for our hatred is pointed only toward today ...
And today's current condition can always be risen above and improved.
Nor will we be trapped in our old personality, or the condemnation it felt.
However if we ignore the maternal Holy Breath of Divine essence and Mind
(our creative intelligence and purifying power)
We're ignoring our Inspiration, Intuition, and Conscience,
And we are breaking our own personal trust.

When we do not practice breathing the Sacred Breath, for its purification
process, we are ignoring the powers of growth, transformation, and healing
in our life, and we're pushing away the nurturing
Divine Hand in daily moments.

All this Love *is given freely to us so that we may rise up* into our true self in
unhindered Grace, **while on Earth,** to rise above the physical tomb of ego.

The Holy Breath-spirit is our facility that expands our human awareness
and transforms our body to light.

Our breath allows ascension out of the down-pulling
ego tendencies that enslave humanity.
We might as well banish ourselves to the "far country" of sorrow
for turning away the maternal "*helping hand of breathing the Breath-Spirit*"
and its loving guidance.

Whenever the igNorance of our Holy Breath occurs,
and its powers of purification and its inner inspiration are absent
from the mental and physical activities of our life,
they are also missing from our **Conscious Spiritual Awareness**.

How then can this *ig-Norance and Refusal* of Divine Guidance
be *'for..Given'*
in either the material realm of the body, or in the etheric realm
of our consciousness, when…
[it is not even received] … or practiced?   44.

XI

The Solitary One:
In the Light

"Be still ... know ... I AM God."
~Psalms 46:10

*B*lessed are the ONES who have unified their Intention, Attention,
and Expression with divine solitude — [the SOLITARY];
and blessed are "the Elect,"
[those consciously dedicated to their divine reunification]
for they shall live in bliss, in their true Home, in eternity and light,
and they shall find rest in their Original Soul awareness. 49.

They said: "Lord, there is so much mental advice regarding
our subconscious mind.
And this religious input sounds holy and seems spiritual, but there's no real
help from it, for removing the ache within our heart, nor for truly assisting
us to ascend out of our mental discontent, which we constantly endure
[*in the emptiness that our ego-mind continually experience*s]." 74

He replied: "Yes, there is help... *transformation deserves assistance,*
but truly anointed *Christed* Teachers are scarce.
So in prayer see, and joyfully feel, the I AM sending your Light Self
into your ripened heart...to rebirth and breathe you,
— another Divine Child — who is ready for The Change." 73.

A woman from the crowd said to him:
Blessed is the womb that gave you birth and the woman that nursed you."
He replied: "Blessed are those who have heard the Word of the I AM
and heeded that pure Christ Awareness within,
and who have obeyed The Word, maintaining themselves in Truth
through maintaining attunement with their Deep Self.

This Word 'I AM' is always near you.. in your mouth and in your heart,
so that you readily may find it and experience its
transformational, guiding power.
A day will come when many will say:
'Blessed are the barren or childless ones,
who used the time that would have been spent raising children
to enter their Expansive Light Being within
and have given birth to their Spiritual Persona instead.' 79.

Any one who does not turn toward the inner I AM – surrendering the
earthly father and mother, and brothers and sisters of this world,
   — not giving up their old ways, taking up their "cross," as I did,
   — not putting away their former life, giving up their old routines
   — but seeking their Original Life Force instead—cannot become worthy
of ME — their Whole Self. For it takes reorganizing, one's life-priorities.

The journey requires a dedication to interiority
and a *single-minded attention* to achieving the pure and permanent Identity.
Remember, one who travels alone, travels far.

So if we let our family pressure us, or lead us away from the inner pursuit
of our solitude experiences,
we cannot enter into our wondrous and powerful Self Awareness. 55.

In nature, foxes have lairs, birds have nests, and everything in the world
has its own place. However, the spiritually born offspring of humanity—
the "Sons of Mankind" – those newly transformed Children of Light
and new members of Earth's Divine Race – have no 'worldly' thing
in which to Rest their mind, [*providing spiritual nourishment*]
as *focusing on* our Divine *Consciousness* does.
For their contemplative home, is in the "I AM Light"
and they are merely transients of this beautiful world
and its dualistic hypnotic system.   86.

Mary Magdalen said to Yeshua: "*Tell us what your disciples are like
and how they should be in the world when you are gone.*"
Yeshua replied: "Their life is like a FARMER [one with a spiritual path]
who discovers STRANGERS [temptations] traveling through,
and they camp in the FIELD 'of his heart.. where they do not belong'.
And when the *Farmer of the FIELD* [disciple] discovers these temptations,
he orders them *Out of his heart-space,* so the intruders quietly depart,
leaving his mind and heart-space unburdened."

So be as wise in this world as those who are users of the system.
If someone knows to expect trouble before it happens,
like expecting a THIEF at a certain place and time,
[*like a temptation which regularly arises in one's life*]

then be prepared against the dangerous entry,
block the way and protect your consciousness from ***painful mistakes.***

Be wary of the world system, with its dominating influences
and its down-pulling temptations, persons, and attractions.
It will make you its brother and its honored guest.
And then like a THIEF in the night, it will rob you blind
in your unsuspecting darkness. Therefore, prepare yourself daily.

Seek your divine Awareness Early, in your day and in your life that you
may always feel the Presence within, while you work and while you play.
When you go in and go out in all your activities, maintain this
watchfulness on the Inner Presence, and it will lead you and live through
you as you, and you shall feel insight and power that is humbling.

Ever before you sleep, graciously and with gratitude Surrender the
operation of your consciousness [temple-path] to your all-knowing Self,
that Original Soul Spirit Expression whose divine right is to live this life,
that you thought belonged to your ego-habits and daily patterns.

It is up to you to surrender the past of the ego personality.
It is up to you to willingly release your consciousness back to your I AM,
before you sleep at night, with consent and harmony.
Let it be like keeping an appointment with a lover, that is honored tenderly.
Go to rest at night with loving gratitude, and rise up each day
in partnership with Divine Being.
Practice this Presence ceaselessly throughout the day, and have patience
toward yourself and your efforts.

Let no self-condemning judgment rise up in you, but stay in balance,
even with life's vicissitudes.
This being done, you shall be lifted up and exalted with the Highest,
and you shall live life in grace, with abundance and peace.

No THIEVES [no ego impulses] shall enter your being to steal
your confidence or destroy your tranquility ... for you will be in the Power.

So be as zealous in your pursuits, as the children of darkness are in theirs;
for the benefits you expect and the fruits you anticipate
from walking the spiritual path will be found.

So... "How do you live in this world ..?
And what does the Lord Require of you?" It's Simple.
Do justly, Love Mercy, and at all times humbly Walk with Your God within
— by attending to the graceful feelings of bliss within you.

May there arise within you a WISE ONE [*your portion of your Holy Breath*]
which will manifest in this world, as our True Self, when It is ready
and while we are still within "Time".
Let him who understands, act, asking his inner Lord to transform him
when his 'time' is ripe. 21.

After this has transpired, if people ask about the origin
of your powerful Awareness, answer:
"*We arose out of the Light of Infinite Awareness, where projected visible*
light came out of itself—out of its Resting State — from its invisible
formless Being; and it "rested from work" in us, as it formed our
"moving image," and our holographic Self Awareness.

If you are asked regarding your spiritual Identity, answer this way:
"*We are Children of the Living Light, and we are the Expressed Image*
emerging from the Living Light of Divine Being."
If ever you are asked what is the sign of Divine Being, answer:
"*Movement and Rest, the In-breath and Out-breath, our Heart Beating,*
— emanation and concealment — the One and the many,
and invisible Life and visible Expression." 50.

His disciples asked him, When will this Divine Kingdom come
and cover the whole earth and everyone therein. Yeshua said:
"God's Kingdom [Consciousness] will never come as an observable event
the way you are expecting it.
No one will ever say, '*Look, there! It is arriving,*'
or 'Look over here in this mountain. It has finally come.' [Q]

Because the Kingdom of God is not a visible appearing.
It is within you ... invisible to human eyes.
"It is the spiritual guidance of Divine Being within, that transforms our
heart and our actions. It arrives in each of us in our own time. Gradually
this Kingdom increases on the earth plane, as each one of us manifests its

Presence, day by day, first one, then another, then the whole; but it is You who points yourself toward its entrance, and it is You who walks in.

The invisible governing Power of I AM and its omnipresent spiritual Consciousness is already spread throughout Heaven and Earth, sustaining everything, yet no man sees it.
It is seen in the masterpiece of the Universe, *its visible expression.*
It does not even need to arrive, for this Kingdom is here right now.

So unless you pursue your spirituality and are dedicated to arriving in the consciousness of bliss and power, in your inner I AM,
this Divine Heart and Consciousness will remain invisible to you.
You must *feel* this Awareness.

To feel it you must go back into the Deep of your Consciousness.
You must be born from Above in the renewal of spontaneity in your life,
seeing without predisposed expectations or negative thought-taking,
just letting go the past.
This way you will perceive freshly the purity of each now-moment,
and you shall cleanse your moment-to-moment fluid Awareness
of all worldly identifications by continually focusing inward
on that pure awareness;
and you shall daily **raise the quality** of your Sea of Consciousness
through contemplative meditation, experiential visualization,
and consistent heart-felt prayer — dedicated to you and Everyone.

For what you can give to another, you yourself can also receive.
Doing these things will transform the thought projections
of your human heart, where they originate and live.
You will feel and think from a higher vibration.

And once accomplished, you will rise higher in the Consciousness of bliss.
Also, you must be "born" a 2nd time in the Divine Breath — born in the realization *that your Conscious Breath* is God's Movement and Rest in you.
In the spiritual life, it is known as.. the "purifying fire."
When you know that this Breath is your bodily connection to the *infinite Living One*, and along with consciousness, is your portion of Divine Being,
then you shall experience the "fire of transformation"
and find that Kingdom in your Center, as your life force.

Thereafter, you will always feel the Divine One moving powerfully
as your life. So if you start the journey back, away from your ego nature,
and with a "wave of determination" will dedicate yourself in earnest
to this progress, you shall be met by your Divine Self Awareness,
while you are yet a "long way off,"
and there shall be celebration over your Divine Re-union. [R]. 113.

You see, the Divine conscious essence *envelops us.*
Images of light appear all around us, in every moment of life.
We see these lighted "forms" as 'everything' in our environment.
And there is within these lighted images, a *Living Mind - Presence,*
which is hidden behind the reflected light in
the outer "form" of everything;
however… it Lives and Breathes within "The Travelers" — the beings;
– the "visible" Children of God.
This Divine I AM reveals *itself and its Essence* personally to each of us. 83.

In that day, Divine Being shall be unveiled to you as your inner I AM,
-as your transpersonal heart-level Awareness
and your life will never be the same.
Your inner Image, *of this holographic Light Body,* will be revealed
to your Awareness, and will be Unfurled before your vision…
and you shall know it, as your "body's" *Traveling form.*

Your Identity as a Living One — a traveling Light Child and visible "I" —
will be known by you, To be an Individual Image of the Living ONE
— the Omnipresent I — who is our Resting Infinite Light Being,
and our invisible I AM. *You are the Image and Likeness of Divine Being...*

And you are infinitely loved .. and you are assured in this truth.
If you know this, you will neither see "death", nor know fear ever again.
Realize, this world *cannot restrain the ones* who find their Deep I AM. 111

THE END

the Amplified Interpreted
~ Gospel According to Thomas ~

Author's Note

I have personally found that re-reading spiritual material frequently, over considerable time, has granted a significantly deeper comprehension within, and a transformation of awareness can therefore occur for us. Practicing the Holy Breath unifies us, in a Oneness with our Divine Life Force-Source. Through growing "a movement and a rest" awareness in each moment, at last we Breathe a release of ego.

It comes with endless sighs of grace, and then... Gratitude overwhelms our heart, and expands our Mind and our very Being. This is the gift of The Divine Breath in us... which Yeshua Christ gave to our awareness.

FOR THE VERSES IN THE ORIGINAL VERSION OF THOMAS, GO TO PAGE 149.

THE ORIGINAL
THOMAS
VERSES

1. *Yeshua said:*
Those who uncover the significance of these words
shall not taste death.

2. Let those who seek not cease from their search until they find, for
they will be troubled before they find. When they find, they will be
awestruck and in wonder, and after being in wonder, they will then
reign over the All.

3. If your teachers claim that the Kingdom comes in the sky, the birds of
the sky will be there before you. If they say that it arrives from the sea,
the fishes of the sea will be there before you.
The Kingdom is within you and without you.
When you know your Self, you will be known by others.
Then you shall know that you are sons of the Living Father.
But if you do not know your Self, you are impoverished;
in fact, you are poverty.

4. An old man, heavy with years, will not hesitate to ask a baby, only
seven days old, about the place of life; and he shall live,
for many who are first shall be last, united within the Single One.

5. Yeshua said: If you know what precedes you, then that which is
hidden will be revealed.

6. Disciples asked Yeshua:
Do you want us to fast? How do you want us to pray and
distribute alms?
What dietary rules should we observe in eating?

   Yeshua spoke: Do not lie. Do not do anything you dislike, for all is
revealed before Heaven. Everything hidden shall be revealed.
Nothing covered will remain undiscovered.

7. Blessed is the lion eaten by a man, so that it becomes a man. But
wasted is a man's being who is eaten by a lion
so that he becomes a lion.

8. A man's life is like a skillful fisherman's practice, for he casts his net into the sea and draws it out filled with small fish. If the wise fisherman discovers among them a large fish, he throws the smaller ones back into the sea, having caught the largest one already. He who has ears to hear, let him hear.

9. Yeshua said: A sower comes forth, fills his hands, and casts the seed. A few seeds fall upon the road, where birds come to devour them. Others seeds fall among thorns, where they are choked out, or are eaten by worms. Still other seeds fall upon good ground, where they can bring forth good fruit.

10. He said: I have set a fire upon the world. And I will rekindle it until it burns everywhere.

11. This Heaven shall pass away, and that which is above shall pass away; the dead will no longer live and the living will no longer die. When you digested good things, it was you who gave them expression. But what will you do when you enter the light? When you were one, you became two, but now that you are two, what will you do?

12. Disciples asked of Yeshua: We realize that one day you will leave us. Which of us is to be the leader of the group? Yeshua replied: At the time when you are left, you will go to James the Just, for whom Heaven and Earth came into being.

13. Yeshua said to his disciples: Compare me to someone. Tell me whom I resemble. Peter said: You're like a righteous angel. Matthew continued: Or like a wise philosopher. But Thomas replied: Truly, Master, I cannot bring myself to utter comparisons to you. And Yeshua said to him: I am no longer your master. You have partaken of the bubbling fountain which I brought and you are drunk with it. Then he took Thomas aside and said three words to Thomas When Thomas returned, and his companions asked him: What did Yeshua say to you? He replied: If I told you even one of the words he gave to me, you would take up stones and you would hurl them at me; then fire would leap from the stones and would burn you instead.

14. Yeshua said: If you fast, you will just create sins for yourselves.
    If you pray publicly, you will be ridiculed.
    f you proudly give alms publicly, you will set yourself back.
    If you travel into a region, wandering through its countryside, and are
    offered hospitality, eat the food set before you. Heal the sick among
    them. For it is not what goes into your mouth that defiles you, but
    what comes out of your mouth that defiles you.

15. When you perceive one not born of woman, bow yourselves down
    and worship Him. He is your Father.

16. People think I have come here to bring peace to the world. They do
    not realize that I have really come to divide; to bring fire, and a sword
    and conflict. There will be five in a house with three against two, and
    two against three; the father against the son, and the son against the
    father, and they shall stand alone.

17. Yeshua said: I shall give you what no eye has seen, nor ear heard,
    nor hand touched, nor any heart received.

18. Disciples said to him: Tell us what our end will be like.
    Yeshua replied: Have you discovered your beginning, that you can
    now ask about your end? Where the beginning is, there shall be the
    end as well. Blessed is the one who understands the beginning, for he
    understands the end without tasting death.

19. Blessed is the one who was before he came to be.
    If you become my disciples and respond to my words, stones will rise
    up to your service.
    You have five trees in Paradise, unaffected during summer and winter,
    not shedding leaves. He who knows them all, shall not taste death.

20. Disciples challenged him: Tell us what the Kingdom of Heaven is like.
    He answered: The Kingdom of Heaven is like a seed grain of mustard.
    Although smaller than other seeds, when it falls upon tilled soil, it
    grows forth a great tree, which becomes a splendid home for birds.

21. Mary Magdalene asked Yeshua: What are your disciples like?
    He responded:
    It's like when strangers sit in a field that does not belong them.
    When the owners of the field discover them, and demand,

Get off our field, The strangers will relent, and will hand it over.
So I say to you, in a like manner: Isn't it true that if a householder
is aware that a thief is coming, he will prepare and await his arrival,
block the way into the house—his kingdom---and protect his
property? And so, be wary of the world system.
Gird your loins in strength so that no thieves enter in.
For the benefits you expect will be found.
And may there arise a voice of harvesting, and when your fruit is
ripening, he comes with his swift sickle and reaps your harvest.
He who has ears to hear, let him hear.

22. Yeshua saw some babies being fed by their mothers.
    He addressed his disciples
    These babies being nursed are similar to those entering the Kingdom.
    His disciples asked: We are small. Can we enter the Kingdom now?
    Yeshua said: When you make the two into one, and make what is
    within like what is without, and make what is without like what is
    within, and make what is above like what is below; and when you
    unite male and female in one, so that the male is no longer male and
    the female is no longer female;
    and when you make eyes replaced by an eye, and hands replaced by
    a hand and feet replaced by a foot; and your images replaced by an
    Image, then you shall enter the Kingdom.

23. I shall choose one from a thousand, and two from ten thousand,
    and they shall stand unified.

24. Disciples requested: Tell us about the place where you live, for we will
    seek it if you tell us. He said: Let him who has ears to hear, listen to
    these words and honor them. There is light in a man of light, and he
    gives this light to the world. If he does not give his light, t
    here is only darkness.

25. Love your brother as your own soul. Cherish him
    as the apple of your eye.

26. You notice the particle within your brother's eye, but you do not see
    the beam within your own. Once you've removed the beam from
    your own eye, you can help remove the particle from
    your brother's eye.

27. Unless you abstain from the world, you will not find the Kingdom. Unless you honor the Sabbath, you will not see the Father.

28. I came and stood in the middle of the world. I appeared in a body, and I found everyone drunk, and no one thirsty. Then my soul was sorry for all the children of mankind, because they are blind in their heart. They do not understand that they have come unfettered into the world and will leave it unfettered. Now they are like drunks, but when they renounce the wine, they will understand, and change.

29. If the body came into being for the sake of the breath, that would be a mysterious riddle; but if the breath came into being from the existence of the body, that would be a wondrous miracle. How do you think such great wealth makes its home in such apparent poverty?

30. Where there are three, gods are God. Where there are two, or one, I am with them.

31. No prophet is honored in his homeland. No doctor heals those who know him well.

32. No city built high upon a mountain, and well-fortified, can fall, nor can it conceal itself.

33. Yeshua said: Whatever you hear with one ear and the other too, preach from the housetops. Nobody lights a lamp in order to place it under a bushel or to hide it in some secret space. They set it upon a lamp stand, so all who enter or depart may see its light.

34. When the blind lead the blind, they fall together into the ditch.

35. Nobody can enter a house of a strong man, or seize it by force; unless his hands are tied. Only then can the house be ransacked.

36. Morning to evening and evening to morning, do not think about what you shall put on.

37. Disciples asked him: When will you appear again to us
     and when shall we see you next?
     Yeshua answered: When you shed shame and take your clothes,
     putting them on the ground and then trampling them underfoot like
     children, then you will see the Son of the Living One and you will
     no longer have fears.

38. Often you have wished to hear words like I am expressing to you now.
     And times will come in your life when you will search
     for this inspiration but will not find me.

39. The Scribes and Pharisees received the keys of understanding
     spirituality and hid them. They did not enter into it,
     nor allow entrance to those who wished for it.
     Be wise as serpents and innocent as doves.

40. A vine was planted outside the Father. But as it was never connected,
     it was torn at the roots, and it died.

41. He who possesses a thing in his hands will receive it again naturally,
     and from him who has not a thing in his hand, it shall be taken away,
     even if he somehow gets it.

42. Yeshua said: Be passers-by.

43. The disciples said: Who are you to say that to us?
     He said: You do not understand who I am, from what I say.
     You've become like the Jewish academes. They love the tree and
     hate the fruit. You love the fruit and hate the tree.

44. One who blasphemes against the Father shall be forgiven and he who
     blasphemes against the Son shall be forgiven, but he who blasphemes
     against the Holy Breath shall not be forgiven on Earth or in Heaven.

45. Grapes are not gathered from thorn bushes, nor are figs plucked
     from weeds.
     A good man produces good from his heart's treasure. An evil man
     brings evil from his heart, speaking evil when he expresses himself.

46. Yeshua spoke: From Adam to John the Baptist, none born of woman
is higher than John the Baptist, whose eyes remain unopened.
Whoever shall become small, shall realize the Kingdom and
shall be exalted above John the Baptist.

47. A man cannot ride two horses at the same time, or bend two bows;
and a servant cannot obey two masters, for he must honor the One
and deny the other. And nobody drinks old wine, then desires new.
Nor is new wine packed in old skins, or they crack.
Old wine is not put into new skins, lest the new wineskin perish.
And an old patch is not placed upon new clothing, for it tears.

48. If two make peace with one another in the same house,
they can order the mountain to move and it will move.

49. Yeshua spoke: Blessed are the solitary and the elect, for they shall
discover the Kingdom from which they come, and to which
they will return.

50. If ever you are asked your about Origins, answer: We have come out
of the light where the light came out of itself. It rested, appearing in
our image.
If you are asked of your identity, answer: We are his children, and the
elect of the living Father of Light. If asked for a sign of your Father,
answer: Movement and rest.

51. His disciples asked him: When will the rest for the dead begin?
And when will this new world arrive?
He responded: The sanctuary you're expecting is already here,
although you do not recognize it.

52. Disciples commented: Twenty-four prophets in Israel spoke, all
referring to you. Yeshua replied: You've neglected the one
who lives within your presence, to talk about the dead.

53. Disciples asked: Is circumcision a true benefit? Yeshua answered:
If it were truly useful your Father would have birthed you circumcised
from your mother. But the real circumcision of the human heart has
always been beneficial and nothing but beneficial.

54. Blessed are the poor, for theirs is the Kingdom of Heaven.

55. Yeshua said: He who does not hate father and mother will not be my
    disciple, as he who does not hate brother, sister and family,
    and take up his cross as I did, cannot ever become worthy of 'ME'.

56. He who understands the world's ways has found a corpse,
    and the world is not worthy of him who has found a corpse.

57. The Kingdom of the Father is like a farmer who possesses good seed.
    One night his enemy sows weeds among the good seed, but the
    farmer refuses to pull up the weeds, saying: We might uproot the good
    fruit as well; on the harvest day the weeds will appear,
    will be uprooted, then burned.

58. Blessed is the one who has experienced suffering,
    for he can truly discover the fullness of life.

59. Look to the Living One as long as you live, lest you die,
    then start searching for him, without finding him.

60. A Samaritan was carrying a lamb while on the road to Judea.
    Yeshua asked his disciples why the man carried the animal.
    They responded that the man wished to kill it and eat it. Yeshua
    replied: As long as the lamb is alive, he will not eat it.
    He can eat the lamb only after it is dead.
    They said: There is no other way
    Yeshua responded: You too should be seeking the death of
    involvement with this world, in order to avoid becoming corpses and
    becoming ripe for being eaten up in your life.

61. Two share one bed; one shall live and the other die.
    Salome questioned him,
    Who are you? Have you slept in my bed, or eaten from my table?
    Yeshua said to her: I am an equal. I have been given the things
    belonging to my Father.
    Salome replied: And I am your disciple.
    But Yeshua replied: When one is becoming equal,
    he shall become filled with light.
    However, when one is drifting apart, he will be
    consumed with darkness.

62. Yeshua said: I reveal my secret truths to those deserving of them.
Do not let your left hand know what your right is doing.

63. A rich man with a great fortune determined to employ it, so as to
plant, sow, reap, and to fill his barn with harvesting, so that
he would want for nothing. But, suddenly, in that darkness he died.
He who has ears to hear, let him hear.

64. A host, having prepared a banquet, sent out his servant to summon
the guests. He went out to the first one and said: My master has
invited you to the banquet. But the guest said: Some merchants in
debt to me are visiting me tonight. I have to advise them. I am sorry,
but I cannot come. The servant visited the second and said:
My master has sent this invitation to you for the banquet.
The second guest replied: I bought a house and made my
appointments regarding it; I have no time.
The servant went to another and offered: My master has invited you
to the banquet. He was told by that one: My friend is getting married
and I must organize a celebration dinner. I cannot come.
Then approaching another, the servant said: My master invited you
to the banquet. He answered saying: I have purchased an estate
and must collect the rent today. I cannot come.
The servant returned to his master and reported:
Those you invited are unable to come.
The master responded: Then go into the streets and bring in all you
find to partake of the banquet. Businessmen and dealers do not enter
the House of my Father.

65. A virtuous landlord had a vineyard that he gave out to farmers to be
tilled, and he agreed to receive fruit from the farmers as payment.
He sent his servant to collect the fruits, but he was taken, beaten
and almost killed.
The servant returned, and told his master of it.
"Perhaps they did not recognize him," the master said.
So, he sent another servant; but the farmers beat him too.
Then, the landlord sent his son, thinking, "They will respect my son."
The farmers knew that he was the heir and they seized him too,
and then they killed him.
He who has ears to hear, let him hear.

66. *Show me the stone which the builders rejected.*
    It is the very Cornerstone.

67. *He who knows The ALL but does not know himself*
    has missed everything.

68. *You are blessed if you are beaten or persecuted by others, for they*
    will find no place still left in you, where they can torment you.

69. *Blessed are you, if you have been persecuted in your heart; for you can*
    know the Father in truth. And blessed are the hungry and thirsty for
    this, for their desires will be fulfilled.

70. *When one produces this within himself what he has will save him.*
    What he does not have within will bring death.

71. *Yeshua spoke: I shall destroy this house and nobody will be able*
    to restore it.

72. *A man questioned: Tell my brothers to divide up my Father's things*
    with me. Yeshua said: Who made me a divider?
    Turning to his disciples, Yeshua said: Do I divide things up?

73. *The harvest is great, but laborers are few. Ask the Lord to send*
    laborers to the harvest.

74. *Lord, there are many people around the well. But there is nobody*
    within the well.

75. *There are many at the door, but only solitary ones will enter*
    the bridal chamber.

76. *The Kingdom of Heaven is like a business man who finds a pearl to*
    add to his possessions. Being a clever business man, he sells his other
    possessions, and buys himself the pearl, keeping it alone.
    Seek, like him, that treasure which does not fade, in that place where
    no moths can enter to consume, and no worms to corrupt.

77. *Yeshua said: I am the light that is above all. I am the all. The all came*
    from me; and the all is returning to me. Split wood and I am there.
    Raise a stone and you will find me.

78. Why did you come into the field? To see a reed tremble with the
     wind? To observe a man wearing soft clothing?
     Your kings and famous people all wear fine clothing,
     and yet they do not see the truth.

79. A woman from the crowd said to him:
     Blessed is the womb that gave you birth, and the woman who
     nursed you. He answered:
     Blessed are those who have heard the word of the Father and
     maintained it in truth. For the day will come when you will say,
     blessed is the womb which has not conceived, and the woman
     who has not nursed.

80. He who understands the world has found the body; but he who has
     truly found the Body is too great to be contained within this world.

81. If one is rich, he can become a king in this world; but he who is truly
     powerful cares nothing about it.

82. One who is close to me is close to this fire; one who is far from me is
     distant from the Kingdom.

83. Images appear all around us, and there is light within, which is hidden
     in the image of the Father's light. He will reveal himself and his image
     hidden by light.

84. When you see your likeness, you are pleased. But when you consider
     the images within that do not diminish or approach, how long can
     you stand that?

85. Adam came from great power and great wealth, when he arrived; and
     was still unworthy of you. Had he been worthy of you he would not
     have tasted death.

86. Foxes have lairs, and birds have nests; but the Son of Man has no
     place to lay down his head and rest.

87   Troubled is the flesh that depends upon the body.
     And troubled is the soul that depends upon either body or mind.

88. Yeshua said: Angels and Prophets will make visitations to you,
    and they will give to you what belongs to you.
    For your part, give them, what is in your hand, and ask yourself,
    when they come to receive from them, what is theirs.

89. Why do you wash just the outside of the cup? Do you not realize that
    the person who makes the outside also creates the inside of it?

90. Come to me, for my yoke is light, my rule is gentle,
    and you shall find rest.

91. They said: Tell us who you are so we may believe in you.
    He replied: You are testing the face of Heaven and Earth and have
    not recognized The One before you... but you do not even know
    how to test this moment.

92. Yeshua said: Seek and you shall find. What you asked me recently
    I did not tell you when you asked. I want to tell you now, even
    though you are not asking me now.

93. Do not give the sacred to dogs, lest it be cast on the dung heap.
    Do not cast pearls before swine, lest they destroy them.

94. Those who seek shall find, and doors will be opened
    to the ones who knocks.

95. If you have money, do not loan it out at interest but give it to those
    who will not repay it.

96. The Kingdom of Heaven is like a woman who takes a little leaven,
    puts it in bread dough, and makes large loaves. He who has ears to
    hear, let him hear.

97. The Kingdom of Heaven is like a woman carrying a jar full of flour
    meal on a long journey. When the handle breaks, the meal streams out
    behind her, so that she never notices that anything is wrong,
    until arriving home, sets down the jar and finds that it is empty.

98. The Kingdom of Heaven is likened unto one who wished to assassinate a powerful figure. At home he drew out his sword and practiced striking it against the wall, to see whether his hand was strong enough to wield it.
Then he went out and killed that powerful figure.

99. Disciples said: Your brothers and mother are outside.
Yeshua answered: Those who perform the will of my Father, are my brothers and mother. They are the ones who enter my Father's Kingdom.

100. They pointed Yeshua' attention toward a gold coin, saying: Caesar's men demand taxes from us. He replied: Give to Caesar what belongs to Caesar and give to God what belongs to God.
Then give Me what is mine.

101. He who does not eschew his father and mother here, cannot be my disciple; and he who does not love his Father and Mother here cannot be my disciple. For my mother here gave birth to death, but my true Mother has given me life.

102. Troubles shall come to the Pharisees. They resemble a dog in a cattle barn, who neither eats nor allows the oxen to eat.

103. Blessed is the one who knows the time of the robber's arrival. For he can rise, gather himself, and gird his loins, to prepare himself.

104. They said: Please, let us pray together and fast.
Yeshua said: What flaw have I displayed? Have I failed to do something?
When the bridegroom departs from the bridal chamber, then you can fast and pray.

105. He who believes in his Father and his Mother here, is really an illegitimate child.

106. When you make the two One, you will become Sons of Man. And then if you order the mountain to move, it will move.

107. The Kingdom is likened to a shepherd who owns a hundred sheep, the greatest of which was not there. So he left the ninety-nine in search of the great one, until he found it. After all his trouble, he said to the great sheep: I love you more than the ninety-nine.

108. Those who drink from my mouth shall become as I am.
I shall be like him and him like me.
For him, the hidden things will be revealed.

109. The Kingdom is likened to a man who is ignorant of the treasure hidden in his field. When he dies he leaves it to his son, who sells it, being also unaware of the treasure within it. The buyer will come, discover the treasure while plowing, and lend out wealth at interest.

110. He who has discovered the world's ways, and its riches, should then deny the world.

111. The heavens shall roll back, and the earth shall be unfurled before your eyes. The Living One out of the Living ONE sees neither death, nor knows fear again;
for Yeshua says, the world is unworthy of the ones who find themselves.

112. Yeshua said: Troubles come to the one who looks to his mind for comprehending his life. And troubles also come to those who look to their body to keep them fulfilled.

113. Disciples asked of him: When will this Kingdom arrive?
Yeshua responded: It will never come the way you are expecting it.
No one will say, look over here or look over there, it has come!
The Kingdom of the Father is spread all throughout the earth yet no man sees it.

114. Simon Peter suggested: Mary Magdalene should leave our group.
Women are unworthy of this life.
Yeshua said: I shall guide her to make her as a male, that she may become a Living Soul as you others ... for every woman who becomes like a male shall enter the Kingdom of Heaven.

PAGE / VERSE LOCATOR

THE QUOTATIONS IN *THOMAS*

[A] John 14:19
[B] John 14:23
[C] Acts 17:28
[D] II Cor. 6:16
[E] Matt. 6:26-30

[F] Prov. 3:6
[G] Matt. 6:5
[H] Matt. 6:4, 6
[I] Ascribed to an
     ancient Indian
     Master

For the verses in the original Version of *Thomas,* go to page 149.

[J]	John	3:23	[P]	John	14:10	[U]	Eph.	4:4-6
[K]	II Cor.	6:4	[Q]	Matt.	24:26	[V]	Isa.	26:3
[L]	Matt.	4:17	[R]	Luke	15:20	[W]	Isa.	30:15
[M]	Luke	17:21	[S]	Mic.	6:8	[X]	Kahlil Gibran	
[N]	Psalm	139:2-10	[T]	Dan.	5:23		"The Prophet"	
[O]	John	14:6						

~ Epilogue ~

THE PROMISE OF
'THE DOMINION OF HEAVEN'
IN YOUR LIFE

*T*he Reward for attaining this *Oneness* (this Love shared) – this I-AM-I-ness – is Experiencing and living the Kingdom-icile of God as a Dominion of *Heaven* (expansion) 'on Earth' (in your life).

Yeshua Christ gave us spiritual technologies which we shared in the preceding pages, that will lead us to an entirely different experience of our Life and living; and gives results in a rather Soon time-frame – not entire life times, but in months and years – in your life *now.*

Please Know: this is not 'religion's promise' of a blissful after-life. Your blissful afterlife is assured. As a Divine Being on an Earth-visit [in a dramatic, salient, experiential masterpiece of living and feeling] – you will return to your Divine Soul Essence afterward.

No, this here is a Promise and a Reward for right now. Our reward in our Earth-life-spirituality is not for somewhere else but right here, where we are.

Essenes teach: *"He who builds on Earth the kingdom of Heaven shall live in both worlds"*. It's somewhat like a parallel dimension. The world looks the same, feels the same, smells the same – it IS our planet Earth, and our life, indeed, but there is something extraordinarily different about it all.

Our experience of it is transformed, with a continuing sense of now-moment newness – quiet exultation. Day-to-day life is truly lifted to newness, soaring above our old life.

Our senses are sharper, more in tuned, more alive and more refined than they were before. We see INTO not just Onto. And that is bliss. Our perceptions of self, others, and plants and animals too, have more sublime understanding – deeper realizations into their being, their needs – and we also have compassion for all they go through in life.

Now, All Colors are more *beautiful.* Occasionally an uncanny *perception* of time slowing, reveals a billi-second 'gap' of light and sound in the continuum of our awareness – revealing Reality .. as mere images. Regarding design with angles, shapes, forms, perspective –

we ever balance on the verge of wonder. Beauty is more beautiful.
The human form is seen as a masterpiece of art and science.
Synthesis of mental concepts and understanding the inner or esoteric in
our awareness...comes together effortlessly. Intuition becomes a normal
occurrence. At any moment of our day Spiritual insights unfold on top
of each other continuously. We just know and feel so much more of the
universe than we ever came close to receiving before, as well as in our
internal universe.

It is bliss to sense and feel (*that we comprehend so much of all around us*)
and have such joy in the perceiving, and tender insight toward it all.
Our Smiles just materialize continually.

And one thing that creates immense pleasure and comfort is seeing God
and God's handiwork *everywhere*. We keep saying 'thank you' over
and over. And each time it is said, it's said with a smile of renewed
graceful happiness. It never gets old, this gratitude.

Our business in it and our endeavors work with some unseen hand of
blessing. Abundance is more a *State of Inner Being* but wealth may be
included also. It's a dimension where deals come together.
Other people bless our work herefrom. Our connections, colleagues,
contacts and facilitators seem to blend together for harmony.

There is also a feeling in our body, in our muscles, our organs and our
mind—that feels like a fine essence of 'physical bliss' (*if such a thing can
be understood*) but our bodily being has more Joy streaming through it,
as if it were happier being Itself than ever before. Muscles feel a joyful
humming vibration being used.

Organs emanate a graceful frequency vibration in their work.
The sacred breathing purifies and elevates all the systems within,
making them new. The etheric essence of God is transmuting the old
into a newly refined, powerful purified systems *everywhere*.
And we will only mention here, extended healing in and out, and
extraordinary abilities, that seem to correct or improve things which
manifest In and Through us as we ascend levels of Divine awareness.
Our physical fitness is also unquestioned – it is sought out and *manifest*
through life, while our health and bodily systems live, a state of grace.

We also discover our own personal healing methodology and practice.

When sensing a discomfort, pain, *dis – ease,* or health issue, we simply place quiet focused meditative attention on the inner discomfort, for *10 to 20 minutes* at a time on different days (*if needing powerful healing)* and that issue dissolves to comfort, and invisibility.

We know that our attention on an inner pain is *directing God's Mind and attention to There,* and then where *ever* Divine Attention is pointed, healing occurs. Like night follows day, *attention heals,* and Divine Attention (our focused consciousness) naturally, and always .. rectifies.

And... the most bless'ed wonderful State, of all these, is that we are in communion with our Father-Mother Divine Life Force Intelligence and in a coherent cascading interchange of Love, right here, now.

We are continually talking and communicating to the Divine within .. and The Divine leads us to the right byways, introducing us to a perfect person in our life. Yes, parking places reveal themselves.

So many things just appear effortlessly. The Divine becomes our All-knowing Partner, in moment to moment existence. And what a graceful state of confidence *That* produces In us. And our smiles and awareness of this exquisite Divine Partnership never leave us.

This Kingdom of Heaven on earth *As you, In you,* and your *Life,* cannot be described in these simple words. The words are of little effect. When one *feels* these truths of this Divine Dominion in one's life *(creating grace everywhere in it)* one will know that words are weak. But we still attempt to try, don't we? Yet the pay-off and blessing for living this spiritual path 'in focused Oneness with The One within,' is beyond any compensation that is ever sought out or described.

Enjoy ... and luxuriate
in this *Oneness with your Lighted One Within.*
It's your Destiny .. and your very own Being.
    You may as well get there now .. and *Consciously.*

Let's share an extraordinarily powerful *Holy Breath* exercise. To put it simply, this is for transformational endeavors. Performing this exercise over months or years will transform one's sense of Self, and one's power-base within awareness, toward a Light that is one's Divine nature. And remember, this is meant to be practiced daily our entire life. We do not stop doing this one day as if we have arrived, or finally accomplished something; as if we got all we could from it. The reason? The reason is two-fold. First is we can never Grow in awareness enough. We will always and Ever have more continuing awareness and more enlightenment to accumulate and appreciate.

Secondly, we can never say "I love You" enough to Divine Being, for providing The All, and all the experiences and enjoyment thereof, through eternity. If someone fed you a masterpiece of dining enjoyment every single day would you ever stop saying Thank you? …of course not. These breathing exercises are a way of *embracing and expressing gratitude* to our Father-Mother God. Practicing these exercises also makes US more powerful, capable individuals in whatever realm we may find our self. These exercises also create another truly advanced outlet through which God can perform greater works of love and power in this three dimensional universe; in us. It's in fact increasing the number of *Christ-like individuals* in the environment to do these exercises. The power that one feels, and is changed by — that one IS, humbles us. But there is an ancillary *power and Gift* in performing this loving discipline. Yes, breathing the Breath of God does its awesome work in us, but *the time spent in it* is *a sign* to Divine Being of *your personal Love* God-ward.

Just scheduling the time and endeavor transforms you and your life and God *rewards it.* Performing this breath work effects a change of one's personal understanding toward one's identity. Eventually, one begins seeing one's self more as Light than matter — more as Love than Pain — more as Joy than sorrow. While you do this exercise you may include visualization and/or prayer during its endeavor. In fact, it is advised that you Do this combining of spiritual technologies at simultaneous moments within your practice. This way you empower the whole exercise with an elevated and sacred purpose.

This exercise includes a brief holding and an expelling of the breath for specific durations of time. Let us discuss some ancient words regarding aspects of our marvelous bodily being. *Ida* (eeda) and *Pingala* (Ping-gulah) are ancient words for the Sympathetic nerve-channel / Left side, and the Para-sympathetic nerve channel /Right side of our Spinal column. This Pathway of spinal nerve fibers carries Life Force energy up and down the body each moment. What's amazing is the nerve fiber network covers essentially every three dimensional centimeter of our bodies, making us connected to and sensorily stimulated by the outside world in amazing ways.

I'm constantly in awe that the most insignificant nerve stimulations such as a tiny puff of air is felt distinctly on my bodily form, whether my knee, neck, arm, ankle—it doesn't matter where. Temperature differences are *instantly* felt by us. The tiniest feelings are known. The body is a miracle of 'sensing.' And all these nerve fibers covering our entire physical being are fed by the sympathetic and parasympathetic nerve channels in our spinal column. The life-force electrical energy that travels through our nerve network is Divine and universal power, downloaded into our body, giving us an experience of the three-dimensional universe. Your electrical neuronic energy is one and the same, as the cosmic energy that fills every space, in our entire cosmos. The energy out there is the same energy in here. It is the same Divine Power everywhere, in God's omnipresence, and it's in you.

The left and right nostrils are connected to these nerve pathways. In spiritual disciplines, we are to take command of our bodily and spiritual energies on their Pathway within our body and Being; and that is why we are practicing these exercises. Masters use this 'energy command' for purposes of healing, touching higher realms, and experiencing Higher States of Consciousness. When we breathe from side to side in the manner being described to you here, we are balancing the positive and negative forces within us in the morning and evening (that are caused by the agitated daily forces around us).

When doing this exercise in the Morning one begins breathing through the Left Nostril and In the Evening one begins the exercise breathing through the Right Nostril. This means we hold down the other nostril while breathing in. This breath exercise should be done, as close to sunrise and sundown as possible…but where it's not possible, do not worry over it. It is better to DO this exercise than not to do it. One may also do this exercise at anytime that one wishes. As much time and energy as one dedicates to this endeavor, is as much as one can feel transformational progress.

There is something about the 'control' of the intake and release of the breath that creates our ability to participate in this energy, and sometimes it causes an a*wesome, powerful 'state of expansion', inner heat, and an indescribable loving sense of expanding Radiant Energy* (which sometimes feels like it may "burst" us). One senses and therefore learns about an expanded "State of Beingness" in this kind of exercise; and one may relate to one's self as an infinite Life Force; (*this is perhaps why one feels like one may burst*). Of course it never does burst us, but it feels like it may… however, the immense unexplainable expansiveness of this Power is such that, all we can say after experiencing it, is one is in a state of absolute and thorough humility and awe, at the love felt (*one may drop one's head* *in complete deference*). One just 'beholds' the experience. One simply feels without thought or evaluation, except for Awe. And one may almost lose consciousness during the exercise *(one often could if one did not have a full intention to maintain consciousness)*. But please remain conscious at all times; do not Lose conscious awareness *(don't faint or fall asleep)*. It is the *conscious experience* of this power and inspiration that is meaningful. *In–Spire* literally means to *in-breathe* (and it means '*from God*') and this is what you are doing. So, if during the indraw or Hold of Breath you feel your awareness drifting away to unconsciousness then hold off on the remainder of it a moment, to bring your full awareness back up, then continue.

I will say right now this exercise *Is* a ***most powerful*** one. Let it be said though, that if one goes into this exercise *just 'for the experiences'* one is tainting one's motive, and *The Power recedes away from curious entertainment value*. We must be in here for its expanding, lifting, cleansing benefits not its extraordinary or interesting qualities. If one is seeking *The One* for entertainment, *The One* knows the motivation and will allow one to prove one's self with perseverance and honest seeking, as one is willing to simply receive whatever Divine Being will give to one without an attempt at controlling-demanding it. So, when it happens it happens. We are doing this to be cleansed, not to be entertained. Do it for the cleansing inspirational purpose. Note: when we hold our breath in the exercises here Visualize only Good things Prayerfully. Pausing your Breath is a very powerful moment indeed.

AT SUNRISE AND SUNSET

Now when performing this exercise you Sit with a Straight Back … placing the Spine in an erect position. As we have said, in the morning one begins by breathing IN through the Left Nostril by depressing down the Right Nostril; but, one does this Left Nostril complete Inhale spanning Four Heartbeats…

For example: (One thousand 1, One thousand 2, One thousand 3, One thousand 4);
THEN one Holds this breath IN for SIXTEEN Heartbeats *(One thousand 1, One thousand 2, One thousand 3, etc.)*.
THEN one expels this HELD BREATH over Eight Heartbeats *(One thousand 1, One thousand 2…etc.)*

BUT…one does this expelling through the RIGHT NOSTRIL (during the morning exercise).

Then one draws the next Breath in on the same Four Heartbeat count but this time it is drawn through the Right Nostril (by holding down the Left Nostril)… *and the inhale is immediate with no pause between.*

Remember this…there is no pause between exhales and inhales… always, it is immediate.

Then once again *it is held down there for 16 Heartbeats* and it is released through the opposite (or Left) nostril over an Eight Heartbeat count.

Now here's one very important point. The Eight Beat exhale you may find challenging to accomplish. (*You may find your pushing out the air faster than eight heart beats, but it does not mean you should stop before the eight beats expire*). You should modulate your exhale so it's measured. You'll have to use your diaphragm to push out *till the expiration of the Eight count.* You may even be surprised that you are still pushing out Air!

This Left/Right complete breath pattern is done a total of Eight times in both the morning and evening exercise. This number corresponds to the seven basic Energy centers in the body, and the single Energy center just above the body—over the crown of the head—which connects us to Infinite Divine Being. Called *chakras* in spiritual writing, it is a center of bodily nerve energy (*rotating/spinning moving energy*) built into our Being, and, they are located at seven ascending centers associated with our nerve junctions, connecting to our vital parts and inner glandular systems-array.

So on each of these *eight sets of breaths,* we are bringing the breath down to one energy-center respectively, lowest first, 1st, 2nd, 3rd, etc.; *one on each breath* – and one then harmonizes the energies there during that sixteen beat count. There is an ascending Frequency Vibration to each energy center in the body, and a certain Color associated with it.

The first one is at the base of the spine where all those nerve fibers terminate, before spreading out, and it's called the root chakra. This is also where the 'Liquid Light' *divine fire energy* resides within each of us, and is raised from. This rising energy has an ancient name from in ancient languages called kundalini energy. It is an ancient spiritual essence 'of Light' planted within us by Divine Being (mostly unknown to society, particularly modern society).

It provides an *evolutionary impulse and directive in the individual and the collective.* It is a liquid light, spark of God in each of us. It's this fact that causes some spiritually oriented individuals, like masters, teachers, healers, and Messiahs such as Christ, to be far more advanced, powerful and empowering/uplifting individuals than the unevolved common person. The kundalini energy provides a higher level guidance in soul-advancement, for you the individual (*you are not doing this transformation by yourself with your small fund of knowledge*).

It awakens and provides extraordinary spiritual experiences in us as it does its daily work. Practicing the Sacred Breath awakens and stirs this kundalini Light Energy to rise within your physio/psychic/spiritual being.

It will awaken each of us eventually but it can also be encouraged by us to do its work, through our intentions and spiritual disciplines. It's at the bottom end of the spine coiled like a "*liquid pearl of Light*" and its journey is up the spine, and it awakens/rectifies each chakra's energies as it travels upward. As it does so, it awakens the spiritual nature of the individual and can create a halo of personal energy. We are to consciously participate in raising this Liquid Light energy from the base of our spine up through our body, through each 'chakra center', and release our Individual Energy INTO the Cosmic Energy of *The One,* and mingle ourselves with The One and The ALL of everyone else.

By doing so, we complete our selves. We take on the Infinite Wisdom of The One and the experiential knowledge of our brothers and sisters, who reside within The All as we do. We are freed of the minute parameters and belief systems of the tiny ego-Me, and rejoin the oneness, as an Integral member of The All.

We are inseparable from and necessary to everyone else including *The One* — who is expressing *Us* just as He-She is expressing everyone of us, Yeshua, Buddha, Krishna or anyone else you may name.

Also realize one thing. With each Exhale, you should know, that Poisons are leaving your body. One primary way that toxins leave our cells in our body is through exhalation. This is medical science, not theory. So realize and appreciate that benefit…in each Exhale…you are purifying yourself. The colors associated in each chakra are *red, orange, yellow, green, blue, mauve and white,* in that order upward. These are the colors corresponding to the bodily chakras, and you may see Etheric White or pure essence of light for the eighth chakra, which exists above the head. All these centers are to be empowered by this liquid Light, rectified, balanced and raised up by it.

8th Energy	(etheric)	over the top of the head—is our entry, connecting space to God's mind.
7th Energy	(white)	is inside near the top of the Head — the Pineal-connect-Point to Divinity.
6th Energy	(mauve)	is behind the eye-brows and relates to the Personal Divine (Christ) mind and your Individuality. It relates to the Pituitary gland, and what is called the '3rd eye.'
5th Energy	(blue)	is located in the throat and relates to The Word and Communication.
4th Energy	(green)	is at the Heart and relates to Love.
3rd Energy	(yellow)	is located at the solar plexus and relates to Personal power.
2nd Energy	(orange)	is the sexual or Creative Power chakra.
Root Energy	(red)	is located at the base of the spine near to where the coiled Liquid Light Is.

SO, when one breathes in these breaths and Holds them for 16 beats… one is Seeing and Focusing on the Color and Function associated with each level particularly when breathing At each numbered breath pattern. For example, when one is on the fourth level of this breathing exercise (at the Heart) one sees and focuses on the color Green; and when one is at the 6th level, one focuses on Mauve.. and the function of that particular center, and so on.

However, it is strongly recommended that when one is in the process of counting the sixteen heartbeats at each and every level of this Left/Right breathing process, that one 'sees' a Lifting of one's Light energy Up To and Through the color of the center one is AT, *at that moment,* and then with each of the other levels in the body that one goes through (*as one proceeds upward*). Then, when one reaches the top (eighth) center leading to the Universal Life force, one unites one's energy with The Universal Divine Energy. This way you unite and strengthen your kundalini energy with each of the color/qualities and essential strengths of the respective Chakra centers you move through, as your Kundalini energy moves UP and your centers also are purified and rectified by the kundalini light.

So one should count 16 heartbeats at each Chakra level, in the "16 heartbeat count" *when one arrives there* (during this 'kundalini lifting' exercise).

As one exhales the breath after the 16 count, you 'see' the kundalini rising up and out the crown of the head. This mingles your Kundalini energy with the Universal. So, there are sixteen counts at each of your eight energetic centers. Also remember because there are eight levels, and on the left and right nostrils *both,* it is therefore a sixteen aspected exercise, because you do each level TWICE, for the left and right side.

Of course, in the evening all of this is reversed — starting at the Right Nostril, instead of the left; and as each complete Right/Left pattern is done, one would do it on each of the eight chakra levels in the evening too. This whole exercise takes about 8 minutes, but when you add the warm-up exercises of deep breathing for a few minutes, which are definitely advised…along with prayer, it can become about 18 or 20 minutes at a sitting. This is just one repetition of the exercise; you may do it again and again if you like…and when you add a visualization or Prayer to it with all of the desires or goals you have, and the personal qualities that you wish to manifest in your life, it becomes even more powerful. In fact if one misses out on prayer during this exercise one has missed an enormous and powerful opportunity.

But remember, silence is bless'ed too. Soon enough one will learn the 'time-frame' for counting these 'heartbeats' in each of the three phases, and can replace counting with some I AM affirmation.. or Powerful Visualizations that take the same amount of time as these counts. In other words, the timing can easily become intuitive.

However, it may end up being all you can handle for the first months of this new program to do but one repetition of this breath work (as its influence could be remarkable) but as you become more adept and familiar with this power, you will certainly be able to handle more. There are other breath exercises that you may employ as warm-ups to this sacred power breathing exercise, and here are a few warm-ups that you may practice for 15 or 30 minutes at a time (or longer, when you choose to later on). Don't be 'bashful'.. practice all you like.

Sit still in a straight back position, breathe in normally through your nose four separate times, not shallow, and not big.. but like a normal breath – and then on the fifth time that you inhale, you inhale a very large and very expansive breath. And on its exhale make it a blasting cleansing release. Get out ALL the air in your lungs. DO this 5 Level exercise as described on 5 Separate Repetitions. This will take you a bout 2 to 3 minutes to complete the 5 repetitions.

Next sitting still in a straight back position place your finger on your right nostril depressing it firmly, and breathe in through the left nostril fully, fully, fully – so your lungs are filled up by just the left nostril intake. Then *without a pause or rest depress the left nostril and EXHALE through the right nostril till your lungs are empty, empty, empty. Really Empty.* Then without a pause or a rest keep holding down the left and Inhale in through the right nostril. Then when your lungs are Filled with just the right nostril breath, depress the right nostril again and release it all fully, fully through the left nostril. It is just a Two Way Reverse Exercise. Very Simple.

But…if you do this for 20 to 40 minutes or longer you will be amazed at how and what you feel. And when you pray and meditate during these exercises it becomes very powerful indeed. Remember you are purifying body and cells of all the impurities that come in and find lodging over the course of a lifetime. You are also cleansing your mind of ego tendencies, bad habits, weaknesses in your will, and many more things than we can name. Do it with enthusiasm and humility. *This is a high-speed way to achieve dominion of the ego and the fleshly weaknesses we may have.* You are taking in the Holy Breath-Spirit, and it is having its wonderful, cleansing "way with you". These exercises are given as an opportunity to practice the Breath for its benefits. For some, transformative spiritual technologies like these are familiar, but others may not have been exposed to them before. Although, the sacred power breath-exercise in this chapter may be new to many people. It definitely deserves our attention and application. Enjoy and prosper in it.

"HAHM — HAH" "HISS — HAH"

Please know this. One will find a heavenly calming peaceful pleasure in sitting back with closed eyes to simply breathe deeply and rhythmically. And one will feel the need to shut down one's thoughts and present mental activity. To achieve this just go to *Hahm-hah* some call it *His-Hah.* It is really the "sound" of our breath going in and out. This is a secret to quieting the mind. We "focus" on this sound, to the exclusion of thinking. Just the sound. To quiet the mind, attend to the Sound.

Remember, *Consciousness is the Masculine aspect of Divine Being* …where all planning, designing and meditation occur, on the *what and the why* for our life experience. *The Feminine aspect of the Divine is the Breath and Breathing.* But know this. This Divine Feminine is not "just our breath". WE tend to think of our breath as a kind of nothing. *'It's just that we need oxygen'* we think. No it is our very life and awareness. This Divine Breath is the intelligence in the universe. It has consciousness in IT too.

When participating here we are in a creative, restorative, healing, constructive – *particle by particle, detail by detail-PROCESS-oriented activity...* but it is often and mostly in silence. Meditation is Masculine, Breathing is Feminine. **Breathing is experiential spirituality.** Breathing says *I love you.* Breathing actually *melts your ego processes right away from you.* Breathing purifies us, above everything else in the universe.

The Breath makes us Christ-like. Meditation *is introspective, worshipful spirituality.* Meditation says *I honor you, I do and I will listen endlessly.* Meditation is being one with the Divine masculine mind. Breath work is being one with the Divine feminine Breath/Pneuma/Spirit of the cosmos. Enjoy them both.

SAMPLE BREATH TECHNIQUE IN THE A.M.

Cover right nostril with right forefinger, then INhale a blast of air through the left, count silently to 4: ("one-thousand-one, one-thousand-two, one-thousand-three, one-thousand-four")

HOLD air in lungs, counting to 16: ("one-thousand -one, one-thousand-two...etc., to sixteen)

Cover Left nostril with Left forefinger, now, EXhale thru right nostril, counting to 8: ("one-thousand-one, one-thousand-two... etc.) till empty. Lift finger.

Cover left nostril with left forefinger, and INhale 4 counts thru Right, then HOLD 16 counts, then EXhale 8 counts, as before but now through the left nostril.

ABOUT THE AUTHOR

LACHLEN PAUL FRENCH

*A*chieving degrees in Theology, Communications, Science and Psychology he received undergraduate honors at Ambassador College. Entering the Communications Fine Arts Master's Program at USC, he taught Communication Theory and Speech Communication at university. A champion in racquetball, he played quarterback as well. Over 40 years in the scholarly research of quantum physics, he brings us the science uniting mathematics with consciousness and physics with metaphysics. He shows science reveals the mystery of cosmic-energy composing everything in the cosmos, including our very consciousness. In this fact he shows methods for re-identifying awareness away from ego through a depth-consciousness, in ancient experiential technologies which have been mostly forgotten.

His written credits over 19 years of writing include: *Christ's Mystic Secret Returns; Breath of Light; Darwin's Fatal Admission; Splendorous Light Within; God, Einstein, Existence, Cosmos, Life, Love, You;* and 11 years in full retranslating for our modern minds the ancient scroll of Thomas. Discovered in 1945 after nearly 2000 years buried in Egypt's sand, he's written the 21st century translation: *The Gospel According to Thomas - Christ's Recorded Sayings of Mastery* (Top of the list on Amazon). He's also written 4 epic screenplays as well: *Mystic Traveler I-III & Aquarian Effect.*

The famed spiritual writer-teacher, William Samuel was his mentor and coincidentally his relative. Earlier he was the public speaking voice for the Barksdale Self-Esteem Foundation in California delivering seminars on realizing, and living true self-esteem. He started three firms in service industries, and was involved with one of the businesses going public. Today he remains a writer and public speaker uniting science and metaphysical awareness, inclusive of the realm of film making. His Beloved ... and adult children fill up his heart.

LACHLEN PAUL
FRENCH

Dear Friend,

I hope you've enjoyed this book, and that it's impact was beneficial. Marketing is never as effective as it's cracked up to be – never as effective as "word of mouth" - coming from real, ancillary sources. I'm very interested in hearing from you in a brief email, simply sharing your response regarding the few questions below.

- Did this material have value to you and your life?
- What did this value look like to you?
- Would you recommend this material to others?
- Would you enjoy your thoughts being shared with others, either anonymously, or not.. for their benefit?

I would love to hear from you. Click on "Contact Us" at **www.booksinthelight.com**

It's been a true pleasure sharing.

Warmly,

Lachlen

17461524R00111

Printed in Great Britain
by Amazon